Humanism

211
S

THE
HUMANIST
EVANGEL

THE
HUMANIST
EVANGEL

by LUCIEN SAUMUR

Prometheus Books

BUFFALO, NEW YORK 14215

Published 1982 by Prometheus Books
700 East Amherst Street, Buffalo, N.Y. 14215

Library of Congress Catalog Number: 81-85573
ISBN: 0-87975-172-X

Printed in the United States of America

CONTENTS

PART ONE

THE HUMANIST IDENTITY

1

THE CRISIS OF IDENTITY

It is indisputable that something called "humanism" has had a long and distinguished presence in history. Humanism can boast of many famous names in every field of intellectual endeavor. There has been a whole litany of these names throughout history, and they cannot be mentioned without suggesting immediately and specifically the concept of humanism.

These individuals are considered to be humanists because, in one way or another, they proposed a vision of self-confident persons in a continuing struggle to free themselves from ignorance and to promote the conquest of knowledge. They are considered humanists also because they searched for beauty or toiled to create it and to surround themselves with it.

For a long time, humanism was a personal endeavor. If there was a humanist "movement," it was reflected in the individual efforts of outstanding human beings who acted out their beliefs in an implicit manner.

Humanists were living in a world that could easily become hostile and they were well aware of it. They were sufficiently resourceful to survive in such a world and to use it to their advantage. Humanists could pretend to be Christians and to work within the Christian context. They were not above using Christianity as a disguise or as a camouflage for their endeavors. They argued about religion, defending those aspects of religion which served to promote humanism against those aspects which threatened it. They subverted the graphic arts, where religious themes became mere pretexts and where the wretched bodies of the Middle Ages were replaced by the beautiful bodies of the Renaissance. This denial of the Christian ideal of suffering was not recognized as such by the contemporary Christians. It is only in retrospect that the humanist ploy is evident.

Although humanism has been relatively free to proclaim itself, now here, now there, during the past two hundred fifty years, it was not until recently that an effort was made to endow it with an organized form and to establish it in an explicit social context. This effort has met with a definite lack of success, and humanism has failed to crystallize into an effective applied system.

Yet, in the face of its failure, humanism is surrounded by resounding successes which should excite envy and be the cause for much puzzlement. There is no need to detail the many triumphs of Christianity and Islam, of Communism and Fascism, nor the individual successes of the many, in modern times, who claim a prophetic mission, the free-lance evangelists and the gurus — some of them sincere, others bold-faced confidence men — who attract large and devoted followings and amass substantial fortunes with the greatest of ease. The success of some of these endeavors, which have been launched as larks, has surprised and sometimes embarrassed those responsible for them.

On the other hand, when one observes the public reaction to humanist activity, one is struck by the lack of interest, in particular from those who should be attracted to it. Most often it is those who are antagonistic to humanism who pay attention to it. They do so because they recognize in it a straw man which they can easily knock down to further their own cause. And in so doing, they provide humanism with most of its publicity. For this reason, its critics may be better advised to ignore humanism.

* * *

Why has humanism failed so lamentably as an organized venture when, all around, it witnesses so many successes, including the most outlandish ventures and even some which do not want to succeed? Is humanism intrinsically without appeal? Is it possible that what the humanist has to say is of interest only to a few dedicated humanists? If this were true, then it would be evident that the continued existence of humanism as an endeavor seeking to become an organized reality within society is a dream without hope or justification and that humanism should be allowed to disappear once and for all, and as soon as possible.

But, if humanists are not ready to accept the inevitability of oblivion and if they must continue to believe that humanism is a cause that deserves to survive, then they must first refuse to accept that the failure is due to an intrinsic defect of humanism. They must assume that the failure of humanism is due to identifiable causes that can be overcome. One of the possible causes of this failure, and one which humanists can overcome, has to do with the actions of humanists as humanists. Is it possible that the performance of humanists as humanists is at fault? Or is it mere wishful thinking to suppose that those who pretend to be humanists have failed to represent the true nature of humanism or, even worse, that they have represented it as something it is not?

How then is humanism being represented? The most important fact is that it is not represented by humanists at all. Humanists uncritically accept the popular definition of humanism. And what do the majority of people— who have not given much thought to the matter—consider humanism to be? One has only to raise the question of humanism to find that the majority of people do not see a difference between humanism and humanitarianism and that they define humanism as humanitarianism and use the two words interchangeably.

The idea of this interchangeability between humanism and humanitarianism is not challenged by those who claim to be humanists, but, rather, it is accepted without question by many of those who make up the membership of humanist organizations. These people would be at a loss to state a difference between humanism and humanitarianism and they would be inclined to dismiss the question as an idle one and to concur with the popular conception, or misconception.

But, if humanism is defined as humanitarianism, how then is humanitarianism defined? What is it considered to be? There is little disagreement about humanitarianism being a vague and general feeling of benevolence toward other human beings. But vague and general feelings are a poor basis upon which to build an organization.

The fact that those who claim to be humanists consider humanism to be humanitarianism and that the latter is, in turn, considered to be merely a vague feeling of benevolence is paramount in affecting the makeup and the course of the organizations created to further the cause of what they consider to be the humanist ideal. Thus, having identified humanism as humanitarianism, these organizations tend to welcome as a member anyone with a benevolent feeling. These organizations become shelters for every imaginable stray cause, all based on different and conflicting benevolent feelings. As a final consequence of this policy, communication between the members of such organizations is very difficult. Whenever ten such members get together, they have ten different feelings, from which come twenty different and conflicting interests and opinions, and the organization remains without a truly common interest and with no opinion at all. The meetings of such organizations are boring exchanges of disconnected sentences by participants who do not really listen to each other.

A humanist organization, unable to define itself as anything but a humanitarian organization, finds itself unable to compete effectively with any of the many special-purpose humanitarian organizations. In despair, it accepts the role of a general-purpose humanitarian organization. It is always in search of a "good cause" and is willing to voice its support to all humanitarian organizations and causes.

Such a humanist organization is very vulnerable. It is up for grabs to the most tenacious members and thus becomes a weak echo of some other special-purpose humanitarian organization, while its other members, who have different primary concerns, watch helplessly, and begin to lose interest. These other members will drift away from the organization for lack of interest in the adopted cause. The sponsor of the adopted cause will in turn abandon the organization because it has become too weak and ineffective to serve the purpose. The organization will then attract new members who will repeat the process.

But humanist organizations do not consider themselves as purely-humanitarian in nature: their humanitarian concern is an end which demands a means, and the best means possible, a means which does not allow hesitations or self-doubt. And this means is found in political activity. Thus humanist organizations, in spite of their weakness, do not hesitate to identify their function as being primarily and specifically political.

But, while humanism is represented as a political activity, it is not considered to be a distinct political activity that can be recognized as particularly humanist in nature. The instability of its humanitarian foundation does not allow this, and the only way it can acquire a political character is to borrow one. And there is such a character ready to be borrowed: it is "socialism."

Humanitarianism in politics, which is usually expressed as "social concern," has not been particularly identified with humanism but has always been popularly considered to be the exclusive preserve of those who identify themselves as "socialists." Since humanist political activity is considered to be humanitarian in character, it is deemed to be naturally socialistic in orientation. Thus socialism has been able to lay claim to humanism, while it has become unthinkable that any other political orientation could lay such a claim. And the socialist claim upon humanism has affected and restricted the options open to humanist initiative.

The claim laid upon humanism by socialism is two-pronged. The difference between the two aspects of the claim depends upon whether or not one who claims to be a humanist also claims to be a socialist.

Those who claim to be both humanist and socialist view humanism and humanist organizations as one more manifestation of socialism and as one more means of achieving the socialist aim. But they also view humanism as an entity constantly tempted to drift away from its appointed cause. Thus they are forever vigilant to detect and to denounce the manifestation of nonsocialist activity.

The socialist politician stresses the importance of action over thought. He continually stresses that the thinker, the "philosopher," the dreamer, the ivory-tower dweller, the individual who questions everything, including socialism itself, can achieve nothing that is positive, and may obviously rather be mischievous, and that it is only the activist, the individual who is politically involved, who can achieve anything worthwhile for the cause of humanism. To the socialist politician, humanism, like everything else, can only achieve something worthwhile if it is attentive to the policies and directives of the socialist political party and if it does what it can to support and reinforce them.

Those who claim to be humanists without being socialists nevertheless, and because of their common concern for humanitarianism, often consider humanism to be an ally of socialism and it is as such that socialism is allowed to consummate its claim to humanism.

Inasmuch as such a humanist feels that the function of humanism is complementary to that of socialism and that for this reason the humanist has no alternative but to support the socialist cause, he is irrevocably led to accept that the role of humanism is subordinated to that of the socialist party.

The humanist is then condemned to say "me too" every time the socialist proposes anything, and the humanist organization becomes a mere tool of the socialist politician. Such an organization will repeat the socialist slogans and will be on the lookout to say what will please the socialist politician: for example, it will never miss the opportunity to say a good word about the "working class."

But however much humanists identify themselves with humanitarianism or socialism, or both, subconsciously they cannot be satisfied with their subordinate role and they seek a role which they can claim exclusively as their own. They find this role when they put aside their humanitarian and socialist concerns for a moment and grope to rediscover their origins. They then remember their concern for knowledge and beauty, and they remember how the prevailing religions have often appeared as impediments to this ideal. And thus the humanists conclude that their role should be essentially anti-religious. And this role they then fulfill with unrestrained enthusiasm.

Thus, whatever the indecisiveness of the humanist with respect to politics and humanitarianism, there is one area where existing humanist organizations have no doubt about their stand. It is against religion. If the humanists do not know what they are and what they are for, they certainly know what they are not and what they are against. And they are against religion with a vengeance. The very word *religion* releases vast quantities of adrenaline in their bloodstreams. At a moment's notice, they are ready to challenge their pernicious foe with all their might and to denounce superstitions and myths wherever they may be found. They are militantly atheistic with a surprising lack of restraint. In attacking religion they have found a release from the frustrations they suffer at the hands of the humanitarians and the socialists.

But this role is still not satisfactory. The claim to anti-religion, while being distinctive, is negative, and as such it is insufficient to define humanism. This is so because a thing cannot be adequately defined negatively, by what it is not; it must be defined positively for what it is. To achieve a positive role while being anti-religious, humanists are led to pose as the defenders of science against religion. They do so by proclaiming the rationality of science against the alleged irrationality of religion. Yet in this role they fail to be particularly rational; nor are they particularly effective defenders of science. While they proclaim their rationality, they fail to do exactly what a rationalist should do, which is to give a reason. Their opponents, who are accused of being irrational, often display more rationality than they do: their opponents give more reasons than they do! Because of their obsession, these self-proclaimed rationalists firmly believe that they have cornered the market on rationality. In spite of their boast, they cannot recognize reason when they are face to face with it, and thus they dismiss their opponents without a trial and with further accusations of irrationality and superstition. Dialogue is always difficult, and as a result the humanists are usually ignored and thus remain a small and ineffective self-righteous group.

Those who pose as the defenders of science against religion are oblivious of the fact that they convince no one and that, to the contrary, they create ill feeling and confirm their opponents in their convictions. But why should these humanists care about the effect of their actions as long as they are doing their appointed duty, which is to proclaim the True Faith?

They never stop to notice that they are not performing any better than the most fanatical of their opponents. While they claim that science contradicts religion, their faith in science has the same kind of absolute quality as does the faith that their more fanatical opponents have in their God. They worship science like others worship gods. They could rightly be accused of having enthroned science as a new superstition or as a new myth.

Furthermore, the attempt of humanists to link religion to anti-science and to pose as defenders of science, in the hope of defining itself positively, turns against humanism. While it is true that it is no longer defined negatively, it is no longer defined distinctively either. Thus humanism, in its role as the defender of science, becomes a subordinate part of the scientific establishment. And, because it badly overplays its role, it is often unwanted in this part. Thus, when it is defined as the defender of science, the identity of humanism is no better but worse than when it is defined as either humanitarianism or socialism.

* * *

It is obvious that since humanism can be defined so differently—as humanitarianism, socialism, or anti-religion—it is suffering from a true crisis of identity. If it is to amount to anything more than the puny movement it is now, it must recognize the problem that confronts it and grant first priority to the question of its identity.

This question is very important, because it is only when humanism has clarified it that it may hope to succeed. However, the humanist must not confuse this hope with a guarantee of success. The humanist must seek an identity knowing that he has nothing to lose rather than thinking that he has something to gain: while the acquisition of an identity can give some hope without guaranteeing success, the lack of such an identity will surely deny all such hope and will guarantee failure.

As humanism acquires an identity, there must be no question as to what it is. If there must be such a question, and if there must be discussions about the nature of humanism, then it can only be among nonhumanists and those who pretend to be humanists. And it must be the duty of humanists to enlighten them on this subject.

If humanism must be identified, it is important to examine carefully those things which it is deemed to be and with which it is identified and to determine whether humanism is not something very different, whether it is not in fact exactly what it is not supposed to be!

Is "humanism" then just another word for "humanitarianism"? Is a humanist organization nothing more than a sort of atheistic Salvation Army, moved by a variety of benevolent feelings for humanity and determined to spare no effort to alleviate its suffering?

Why would we need two words, *humanism* and *humanitarianism,* to denote the same thing? Would it not be simpler to retire one of these words? Would the existence of two different words, with identical etymological roots, meaning the exact same thing not be indicative of undisciplined thinking? Would it not be reasonable to find different uses for these two words? If *humanism* means *humanitarianism,* do we not have two words with one meaning, and possibly a meaning without a word?

If humanism must not be humanitarianism, then must it be a political option? Does *humanism* mean *socialism* or a particular manifestation of socialism? Is humanism the atheistic branch of the Social Democratic Party? Is it just another more perfect socialist party for the pure, a party which must be forever condemned to live in the shadow of its big unwashed brother?

Or is humanism science? Is humanism the Secular Inquisition of Science, whose function it is to scour our society to detect and denounce those who fail to accept and respect the dictates of scientific orthodoxy? Does the scientific community really need or really care for such an arm and such an ally? Is it not more embarrassed and annoyed by scientific fanaticism? Do scientists really care if anyone gets comfort from reading his horoscope? Is there no scientist who, after a hard day's work and while relaxing and reading his daily newspaper, will not glance at his horoscope and half-believe the solace that it dispenses? Are there no competent scientists who believe in God and in a divine creation?

Before deciding what humanism is, would it not be reasonable to look at what was originally considered to be humanism to see if it conforms to the meaning which is now being ascribed to it? Is this original meaning not now without a word to name it? Did the humanists of old, those individuals, who we consider to have been humanists, proclaim "the brotherhood of man"? No. They did not endeavor to help the poor, the oppressed, or the downtrodden. They did not establish hospitals or soup kitchens or orphanages. Nor did they fancy themselves as Robin Hoods who must steal from the rich to give to the poor.

No, these humanists were recognized as such because of the way they lived. They lived in a way that proclaimed a principle about their nature and their purpose. They challenged the belief that human beings are condemned to suffering and ugliness and ignorance and fear. They proposed that it was possible for them to enjoy well-being and beauty and knowledge and peace, and they proved it by the way they lived. Is this not different from a feeling of brotherly love for all people, and is it not deserving of its own name? Rather than be encumbered with a redundant word, should we not restore its original meaning to humanism?

But then if humanism cannot be defined positively as humanitarianism, socialism, or science, must it be defined negatively as anti-religious? Is humanism just an "anti-religion"? Must it be anti-religious because it is opposed to some religions? Was Christianity an anti-religion because it fought so bitterly against the religion of Islam?

What is it that proposes to explain human nature and purpose if not a religion? Is humanism not in fact a religion? Why can it not be so even though it is competing with other religions, with every other religion?

Is it not only as a religion that humanism can have an identity? Is it not only as a religion that humanism can be defined simply and clearly as something distinct from everything else? That it is not a duplicate of something else? That it is defined as something positive rather than as what it is not: that it is defined for what it is *for,* rather than for what it is against?

Evidently, humanism, being a religion, can be classified with other religions. It shares the essential characteristics of a religion. But it is not those other religions: it is a religion essentially different from every other religion, it is itself; it has an identity. And it is in describing this essential difference that the identity may be defined.

2

THE RELIGIOUS IDENTITY

A religion may be described as a system of beliefs about human nature and purpose and as a subordinate system of practices which are derived from these beliefs.

Religious beliefs may be more or less fundamental so that some beliefs are consequent upon others and are less important. Different religions may share some of their beliefs and yet may differ about others. Inasmuch as a group of religions agree about the same beliefs at a certain level of fundamentality, these religions may be said to belong to the same class of religions.

The system of beliefs of a religion or of a class of religions must be founded on a principle which expresses, in a simple, concise, and clear statement, something about human nature and purpose as viewed by this religion or class of religions.

Orthodox Christianity, for example, is a class of religions whose system of beliefs rests on such a principle. The orthodox Christian believes that human beings are creatures of God and that they offended their Creator, who condemned them to eternal damnation and then offered them an opportunity of redemption through the atonement of Jesus Christ. Underlying these beliefs is the principle that human beings are sinners by nature and that their purpose is to save themselves from perdition.

No religion can exist without offering a similar brief and concise declaration which must contain an implicit or explicit account of human nature and purpose.

The principle that underlies a religion should be unique. There is no need for a list of principles: one is necessary, but one is enough and two are too many. The singleness of the principle is desirable to any successful religion. Principles are "starting points": a religion which endeavors to have more than one starting point is courting self-contradiction and failure.

Lengthy "declarations of principles" do not contain true principles but are rather lists of conclusions and corollaries of the true principle. In pretending to be principles, such declarations dilute the expression of the principle and as a consequence this principle will not be recognized for what it is and the religion will lack forcefulness in its pronouncements.

If religions may be classified in accordance with their beliefs, they may also be classified in a more fundamental way in accordance with their principles. But then what distinguishes one principle from another? And what is the greatest distinction between these principles? We propose that this distinction is what distinguishes humanism from every other religion and that humanism is not only a religion but also a class of religions and that the humanist principle defines a class of religions. We further propose that the humanist principle is so fundamental that there are only two classes of religions at this level of fundamentality: they are humanism and anti-humanism. And there are only two most fundamental principles: they are the humanist principle and the anti-humanist principle. Finally, we propose that the humanist principle is tautological in defining human nature and purpose and that the anti-humanist principle, which is in contradiction to the humanist principle, is then self-contradictory: in other words, we propose that the humanist principle is true and that its opposite is false.

What then is the principle at the heart of humanism? What is this principle implied in the lives of those individuals who are said to have been humanists? What is this principle which defines human nature and purpose in a tautological way? Humanism proposes that it is that *the nature of human beings is to seek their own good and that each individual has no purpose unless he is himself his own purpose.*

The humanist principle is not applicable to human beings alone but also to every animal, and it is applicable to human beings because they are animals. Again, it is applicable to animals because they are conscious beings, and it would be applicable to conscious beings who were not animals, if there were such beings. And the difference between human beings and other animals is that human beings can become confused about their nature and purpose, while other animals are not confronted with this difficulty. And therein lies the whole purpose of humanism, which is to allow human beings to overcome this confusion.

When we propose that the humanist principle is tautological, we propose that this principle is the only intellectually defensible one. It is not intellectually defensible in the sense that it can be proved, but rather in the sense that it cannot be disproved. The humanist principle is so singular and different from that which is proposed by every other religion because it alone finds human purpose *inside* the individual. When a religion seeks human purpose in the infinite variety of what is *outside* the individual, it must prove why human purpose is here or there. Humanism proposes that human purpose is not here or there but that it is in the only place which is not here or there, which is within the individual.

Each individual must apprehend the principle privately by introspection. Any individual who claims that his own introspection rather disproves the principle is claiming such a fundamental difference of experience from the individual who claims the opposite that he could only be said to live in a literally different and opposite world, a sort of "anti-world." These two persons would live in such different worlds that they would be incapable of communicating with each other. But humanism proposes that such an anti-world and its inhabitants are absurdities which cannot exist.

Yet most people fail to recognize the humanist principle and appear to live in such an absurd world. This is because the humanist principle is so simple and all-pervasive and they are so accustomed to it that they fail to notice it. Hence the principle seems not to exist.

But those who listen carefully will hear a principle which reveals that our society is schizophrenic. They will hear the principle which our society accepts implicitly while denying that it does. They will hear the implicit moral principle of our society which is in contradiction with its explicit moral principle. They will recognize that the implicit morality of our society is the humanist morality, which is the only true morality, and that the explicit morality of our society, which is the anti-humanist morality that denies that an individual human being is his own purpose and that he must seek his own good, is in fact immorality.

Thus, as the humanist explains his principle and his morality, as he must do to those who are listening carefully, and as he reveals the self-contradiction of his opposite, the truth and value of his principle and morality will be shown to be indisputable.

But most religions should not be considered as humanist or anti-humanist, but rather as nonhumanist. This is so because most religions do not state directly that an individual is not his own purpose but rather state that something other than himself is the purpose of the individual. In so doing, they may appear to state the anti-humanist principle indirectly, but they do not: they have not denied that an individual is his own purpose and they may even believe that he is. This is possible because a human being may have more than one purpose, so that he may have many secondary and immediate purposes which are not himself while he remains his own primary and ultimate purpose. The nonhumanist religion is such because it has lacked sufficient fundamentality to be concerned with the primary and ultimate purpose of human beings and because it has been satisfied to be concerned with one or more secondary and immediate purposes only. Thus it does not contradict the humanist principle because it has failed to address it.

Such religions are confused by the humanist principle because they have failed to give it enough thought. For this reason they will sometimes recognize it as their own and they will sometimes deny it. And it is inasmuch as it more or less recognizes the humanist principle that a religion is more or less true. Inasmuch as a religion recognizes at once and in turn the humanist principle and the anti-humanist principle, such a religion reflects the schizophrenic condition of our society and is in contradiction with itself. This is true, in different ways, of many religions and in particular of many sectarian components of Christianity, and this is why Christianity is not a fundamental religion comparable to humanism.

Once we recognize that humanism is not only a religion and more than a religion but also a most fundamental class of religions, it is easy to see how wrong it is to identify it as nothing more than socialism, humanitarianism, or science. But it is not enough to say that humanism cannot be those things; we must also emphasize that humanism cannot be qualified by those things. Thus it is meaningless to speak of socialist humanism, or scientific humanism, or any other kind of humanism. When one implies that there are different kinds of humanism, one is compelled to evaluate the different kinds. Then humanism can only be defined through long rambling descriptions and explanations which always appear to be inadequate.

If humanism must be defined adequately in a concise fashion it must not allow itself to be qualified. There must be only one kind and quality of humanism. There must be no better humanism or worse humanism. It is not humanism which must be qualified but it is everything else which must be qualified by humanism. Thus, while there is no lesser humanism, there may be lesser or greater politics or religions inasmuch as they are more or less humanistic in principle.

*   *   *

If anti-humanism is founded on a self-contradiction, then what makes this self-contradiction and anti-humanism possible? Why are people so capable of self-contradiction and, particularly, capable of the anti-humanist self-contradiction?

The answer to these questions must be found in the nature of human language and in the fact that it is as easy to say that "A is not A" as it is to say that "A is A." It is as easy to say that an individual's nature is not his nature and that his purpose is not his purpose as it is to say that they are. Thus it is only through language that self-contradiction has entered the world. When Adam sought to acquire the knowledge of good and evil, he must certainly have sought to learn to speak.

But language must not be considered as a curse upon mankind. It is rather a blessing. It is the faculty which makes human beings what they are. Without language, human capacity would not exceed that of other animals. In fact, because of physical limitations, the capacity of human beings to compete and survive would probably be much less than that of other animals. It is probable that without language human beings would be nothing more than frightened wild beasts which could only survive in the most benevolent environment. And such a paradisiacal environment exists nowhere on earth, except perhaps on a few small isolated permanently temperate islands.

If language is such a powerful faculty that it has given mankind the power to live outside of the garden of Eden, it is also a dangerous faculty. It is a faculty which may be misunderstood and, as a consequence, which may be misused and abused. But such a powerful faculty cannot be so mistreated with impunity. It will avenge itself by plunging the offender into a hell of confusion and contradictions. Thus mankind can be afflicted as no other species of animals.

But why must people misuse and abuse language? It is because they cannot avoid doing so. It is because they must learn to use language through a process of trial and error and, for this reason, it may be impossible for them not to misuse and abuse language, in one way or another, at one time or another.

Because language must be learned, it is first a social function. Each individual can only learn his language from others, and he could never have spoken if it had not been taught to him. An individual whom society had not taught to speak would at best express a few primeval grunts. It is reasonable to impute that it is these grunts that have evolved into human language. It is possible that language has developed together with mankind and that, as proto-human beings, and then human beings, grunted at each other and learned the meaning of each other's grunts through generation after generation, human languages evolved into what we know today.

But no individual and no generation can invent a language. And thus, although mankind has created language, the potential of language exceeds the capacity of every individual and of every generation of people. And it is because of this limitation that every individual, more or less, misuses and abuses language. And just as society teaches individuals to use language it also teaches them to misuse and abuse language. It can teach the individual that his nature is not his nature and that his purpose is not his purpose.

But as the potential of language exceeds the capacity of any individual or any generation of people, every individual is capable of finding potential that others have not seen. As each individual becomes more familiar with language, he comes to feel that he can use it better than others do. Thus, while society may tell the individual that he is not his own purpose, this individual is not hopelessly condemned to this belief. This individual can come to contradict society and to recognize that he *is* his own purpose. And, if humanism is to succeed, it must help him in this task. And it must do so by helping him to recognize where he is misusing and abusing his language.

*   *   *

Language is misused and abused when it is used meaninglessly and illogically. To speak logically is, by definition, to speak without self-contradiction.

The self-contradiction, which constitutes the illogical use of language, is clearly the crudest abuse of language. And the crudest self-contradiction is certainly the explicit self-contradiction. But explicit self-contradictions are rare: few individuals will willingly utter self-contradictions except in a rhetorical manner, merely as the mock self-contradictions which are paradoxes and which is a game of daring of which people are fond but which unfortunately sometimes leads to accidents by lulling the players into true self-contradictions.

But more frequent than explicit self-contradictions are implicit self-contradictions which are not obviously self-contradictions and which may be uttered unintentionally: because such self-contradictions are not always obvious to everyone concerned they must be explained by a process of analysis. Implicit self-contradictions may be revealed for what they are when they are transformed into explicit self-contradictions. An implicitly self-contradictory statement is such because it contains one or more words which are not well understood, and it is by substituting definitions for these words that it is possible to transform this statement into an explicitly self-contradictory statement. This process ultimately leads to statements which are couched in simpler and more fundamental words, which is certainly not a bad thing in itself. The ultimate form of the self-contradictory statement, when it has been made explicit, will be to state that "what is, is not." And the only way to respond to such a statement is to contradict it by simply stating that "what is, is."

But self-contradictions are not the only misuses of language. People must use language to speak meaningfully, and the fact that they are no longer speaking in self-contradictory terms does not prove that they are speaking meaningfully. To speak meaningfully is to make a statement that imparts some knowledge about something by stating something else about it. Of course, the self-contradiction is less than meaningless: it does not impart knowledge, it attempts to withdraw knowledge!

If there is a statement that is truly meaningless, in that it neither withdraws nor imparts knowledge, it is the tautology. As a thing cannot be its own meaning, the tautology is the most truly meaningless statement, which is why it is a misuse rather than an abuse of language. And yet the humanist principle is tautological! And as such it reveals the only valid use of the tautology, which is to contradict a self-contradiction. It is only when a tautology is spoken in the absence of a self-contradiction that it is a misuse of language.

Tautologies, like self-contradictions, are implicit or explicit and, again, as for self-contradictions, people seldom utter explicit tautologies. They usually utter implicit tautologies, believing that they are not doing so and that they are really imparting knowledge and expressing something. Such tautologies must be analyzed in the same manner as must be self-contradictions, by the substitution of definitions for particular words in order that they be revealed for what they are.

But meaninglessness is not restricted to tautologies. There is a kind of statement which is not completely meaningless but which is lacking adequate meaningfulness: it is the ambiguous statement which uses words with relative or subjective meanings but which fails to convey these relative and subjective meanings. By default, absolute and objective meanings are assigned to these words. Ambiguous statements are incomplete statements, and most human statements are such in some measure. It may even be impossible to speak without uttering incomplete statements. But in most instances this defect does not matter, since what fails to be expressed is implied and understood by all those concerned; in other cases, the statement is said to express a feeling and no one is really interested in analyzing it further.

Such a statement, which is said to convey meaning but which fails to do so because it is truly incomplete and therefore ambiguous, is the most difficult to recognize for what it is. Because it is so prevalent when it does not matter, it is often overlooked when it does matter. If ambiguous statements are to be avoided, it is necessary to recognize the key words that must always be used in a relative or subjective context and to specify the exact relative and subjective context in which they must always be used. When this is done, it is then possible to analyze those statements where these words are found to ensure that they are used in the proper context.

But ambiguous statements are not the only kind of statements lacking in adequate meaningfulness. Just as it is possible to abuse language by uttering self-contradictions, it is possible to abuse words by using them in a context which may be relative and subjective but which is still a context where they do not belong. People have always enjoyed using language in this manner and speaking metaphorically, and there is nothing wrong with this exercise as long as they are aware of what they are doing.

But metaphorical speech, like ambiguous speech, is second nature to human beings and they are so accustomed to it that they are not always aware of it and not always able to appreciate by themselves that they are speaking meaninglessly. However, as they are made aware of this problem, it becomes relatively easy to analyze metaphorically meaningless statements and to point out those words which are being misused.

Thus, self-contradictory, tautological, ambiguous, and metaphorical statements constitute the abuses and misuses of language, and these may be corrected by a process of analysis of statements and by re-examining the definitions, the meanings, and the contexts of the words that are used in these statements. If humanism is to succeed, if the validity of its principle must be recognized and if human beings are to apply it effectively in their lives, then the humanist must promote those corrective methods which will lead to a better use of language.

It is in this role that humanism is so different from other religions. Thus, while it agrees with other religions that many individuals misunderstand their nature and purpose, humanism disagrees with them in a fundamental way in proposing that their failure is due to their inability to use language rather than to their failure to receive a special revelation as to their nature and purpose.

And it is in teaching people how to use language and how to speak logically and meaningfully, rather than in dispensing a special revelation, that humanism fulfills its religious role to lead human beings to appreciate and to live in accordance with their true nature and purpose.

PART TWO

THE HUMANIST PHILOSOPHY

3

HUMAN NATURE

Among the words which are misused and abused and which are of the greatest importance to religion and to humanism is certainly the word *good*.

This word is used inappropriately when it is assumed to have an objective and absolute meaning, while its true meaning is essentially relative and subjective, so that a thing can only be good if it is good to someone or something to satisfy a need. But needs are different for different individuals at different times. Thus different things are differently good for different individuals at different times depending on their different needs at these different times. Thus whatever may be good for one individual may be wretched for another individual or may even be wretched for the same individual at another time. And yet goodness is often presumed to have an objective and absolute meaning whereby each thing is supposed to be more or less good or wretched in the same way for all individuals at all times.

People have come to consider that goodness is absolute and objective because they have been accustomed to speak of goodness with a mental restriction: this is what they do when they say that something is good without saying whose need and what need it satisfies. People have been so accustomed to speak in this way that they have come to forget that things cannot be good without being good to someone to satisfy a need. In fact, they have come to accept that there is an absolute and objective goodness which is a superior goodness and whereby things are better when they are not good to someone and when they do not satisfy a need.

This state of affairs came about because each human being, more than the individuals of any other species of animals, has a multitude of needs. The fact that one has more than one need raises the possibility that these needs are in conflict in such a manner that the satisfaction of one will inhibit the satisfaction of another. The greater the number of needs, the greater the possibility of such conflicts. In the case of human beings, the number of needs is so great that the occurrence of conflicts is unavoidable.

It is because of the situation of conflict that human beings were led to conclude that "what is good for human beings is not good for human beings." This statement is made possible because of the lack of explicitness in speaking of the good that satisfies a need which conflicts with another need. Thus, when it should have been said that "what is good for a human being to satisfy one of his needs is not good for him to satisfy another of his needs," abstractions were made of all the needs in question and it was said that "what is good for a human being is not good for him."

It is, then, in order to explain away this obvious self-contradiction that an attempt is made to separate goodness from human beings and to postulate an absolute and objective goodness, which is superior to ordinary relative and subjective goodness because it is independent of human beings and because things are better when they are not good to someone and when they do not satisfy a need.

But it must be pointed out that it is still a self-contradiction to say that a thing is better if it is good to no one. Obviously, to say that a thing is good to no one is to say that the thing is not good! It is not to say that it is better!

It is up to the humanist to resolve this self-contradiction and to restore to the word *good* its relative and subjective meaning, because it is upon this meaning that is founded the humanist morality which affirms the tautology that what is good for an individual is good for him, and that it is good for him to satisfy a need.

*   *   *

When it is said that something is good to satisfy a need, it is understood that whatever is good is a means to the satisfaction of the need and that the satisfaction of the need is the end to whatever is good.

But human beings cannot always achieve their ends because they do not always know the means to satisfy them and, thus, they must search for these means. They may find these means, with more or less success, by exercising their rational faculty, which is the ability to apprehend the relationship of cause and effect, of which the relationship of means and ends is a special kind.

The rational faculty may not only reveal the means that can achieve a desired end, but it may also reveal where there is no such means and where the end cannot be achieved and the need cannot be satisfied.

But human beings are not only ignorant of the means that would satisfy their ends; they are also often confused about the ends to the means that they are using. This occurs because they are often compelled to pursue some illusive means with such single-mindedness that they come to forget that they are merely pursuing means and that they come to consider the means as ends. Ultimately, they fail to differentiate between their means and their ends and they fail to recognize the precise relationship that links them. As a result, they fail to recognize when the ends have ceased to be valid and, thus, they pursue vague ends which have little or no value, and which therefore are not true ends.

If human beings are to be rid of this confusion, they must also exercise their rational faculty, as they are doing when they are seeking the means to their ends, and they must seek a relationship of cause and effect between their means and their ends; but, this time, they must view the relationship in reverse, in the sense that they must consider the ends as the causes and the means as the effects.

It is self-evident that someone can only want a means because he wants an end, and the want of an end is the cause of the want of the means which is the effect. If human beings are to be morally rational, they must inquire as to the ends of the means that they are using and, having done so, and having stated an end to their means, they must question the validity of that end by asking: "Why do I want to satisfy this need; why do I want this end?"

But this question cannot be answered without changing the nature of this end: if there is an answer to this question, and if an individual has a clear and certain reason to want this end, then this end is not only an end but it is also the means to something else which is its end.

Thus the good may appear, in turn, as the end of one means and as the means of a further end. We may easily understand that the latter end may become the means to a yet further end, and thus it becomes evident that there are series of means and ends where each means is the end of an earlier means and where each end is the means to a later end. In such series of means, each preceding means is only valid as an end, inasmuch as it serves as a means to a greater end. Thus such series of means are also series of progressively greater ends. Thus, as an individual inquires as to the reason for his end, he may be confronted by a series of means and ends so that the question "Why do I want to satisfy this need?" must be asked repeatedly only to reveal that each end is itself a means to a further end and that the question may only be answered by stating "I want to satisfy this need because I want to satisfy a greater need."

But an individual cannot consider infinite series of means and ends. His faculty must stop somewhere and it cannot stop merely to recognize that the limits of the series are an illusion and that there are always further ends after the apparent end of the series. He must stop to recognize an ultimate end which is not the means to a further end.

And what is this ultimate end, and when does someone know that he has reached it? Again, this end will be found when the individual seeks to prove that an end is merely a means. This end is found when an individual, in full exercise of his rational faculty and examining the nature of the need whose satisfaction constitutes the end, cannot find that this end constitutes the means to a greater end. It is when someone asks "Why do I want to satisfy this need?" and when that individual cannot answer his own question by stating that he wants to satisfy a greater need. As long as someone can say that he wants something because he wants something else, what he first wants is a means, and something else, which is the cause or reason for this want, is the end. When the individual can no longer express such a cause or reason, he has reached the end of the series. He has reached what seems to be the cause without a cause, the reason without a further reason.

And the individual who has exercised his rational faculty to the point where he can no longer ask why he wants something, expecting to say that it is because he wants something else, must now formulate another very important moral question, which is: "Do I really want this end; is this end the satisfaction of a need?" In so doing, that individual is not only questioning the validity of his end but also the validity of the means to that end and the validity of the whole series of means that precede that end. It is at this point that someone may discover that there is no need that demands to be satisfied and that, therefore, there is no end and that the series of means is a worthless series which does not deserve to be exercised.

But an individual may also discover that he really wants the satisfaction of the need, that he really wants the end, without being able to express that he wants to satisfy a further need. At this point, that individual can only express himself tautologically and answer the question by saying that he wants the satisfaction of the need because he wants the satisfaction of the need; he wants the end because he wants the end. At this point, an individual has reached the limit of his moral reason: he can no longer see a relationship of means and ends. He does not merely want but he wants in a special way, which is *to desire,* which is to want an end which is not itself a means.

Each individual must decide for himself when he has reached what seems to be the cause without a cause, the reason without a further reason, which is the ultimate end; when he wants in a special way, which is to desire. And what one individual may consider as a means, which may only be wanted without being desired, may be considered as an ultimate end by another individual who affirms that he desires it as such. And while the validity of means has a certain objective quality which is in their ability to produce results and which may be appreciated and judged and questioned by other individuals, the validity of the ultimate end, which is not a means, has no objective quality and is beyond the reach of moral reason and cannot be appreciated and judged for what it is except by the individual who desires it.

But while someone cannot express another need as the reason for his need, this does not mean that there is no reason for it; it only means that there is no *moral reason.* But there is still a cause or reason which is beyond

the moral reason and which is the *meta-moral reason*. An important difference between these two kinds of reasons is in their essential relationship to
the individual. Thus, while a moral reason cannot be truly valid until it is
known with certainty and while human beings are assured of knowing it by
exercising their rational faculty, the meta-moral reason, on the other hand,
is valid whether it is known or not, and it is often not known, and it is never
known with the same kind of certainty as the moral reason. The meta-moral
reason for the need is not itself a need: it is a cause or reason beyond the
need. It is a reason *for the individual* without being a reason *of the individual*. It is *a reason* without being *his reason*. This is why it can and does exist
without an individual's knowledge.

In fact, the meta-moral reasons have been a subject of speculation for
most of human history and it is only with the advances in genetics and biol-
ogy, psychology and sociology, that they have begun to be understood. As
such they are the subject of science rather than religion and are of little
concern to humanism.

The meta-moral reasons for someone's ultimate end rest with the origins
and past life of that individual, and the effects of these antecedents cannot
be changed except with the greatest difficulty. An individual could only
attempt to do so by submitting to an ordeal of new experiences which would
do violence to his feelings and desires and which would create new feelings
and new desires. That individual would only accept to do so if he becomes
aware that he cannot possibly satisfy his needs and desires and that he must
replace them with new needs and desires so that he may lead a more rewarding
life.

But human beings have often been asked to submit to this ordeal, as a
matter of routine, on the pretext that they are essentially rational animals,
that their rationality is in conflict with their feelings, and that rationality,
being a faculty which is "superior" to that of feelings, should be used to sub-
due feelings. Thus, nonhumanist religions have often stressed that "reason
must rule the passions."

But what are these passions which reason must rule if not the needs without moral reason, the needs which are beyond the realm of moral reason?
And how can reason rule that which is beyond its realm? How can moral
reason rule the ultimate ends when it is only the means to discover them and
to serve them? Thus reason must not be the master but must rather be "the
slave of passions," as David Hume has observed.

Thus, while it may be said that a human being *has* rationality, which is
merely a tool that he may choose to use or not to use, it is not enough to say
that a human being *has* passions, but it is more exact to say that he *is* his
passions, which he cannot choose not to be unless he literally chooses to
become someone else than himself. But then he could only do so by not
merely abandoning his passions but by replacing them with new ones, so
that a human being can never be devoid of passions without ceasing to exist.

* * *

But each individual has not just one but many needs at the limit of moral reason, none of which can be explained except tautologically. These various needs are often in conflict with one another so that the satisfaction of one will inhibit the satisfaction of another.

Thus each individual must evaluate each of these needs and compare those that are in conflict so that he may choose to satisfy those that are greater to the detriment of those that he has judged to be of lesser importance. But as a result of this exercise some of his several ultimate ends cease to remain ultimate, and as an individual sacrifices the satisfaction of the lesser needs to that of the greater ones this sacrifice becomes the means to the greater ultimate end.

But people often fail to evaluate accurately their conflicting needs and thus choose to satisfy the lesser. And this comes about particularly when time is a factor and when an individual must choose between the satisfaction of an immediate need and that of a different and later one. In such a situation, an individual will be inclined to satisfy his immediate need to the detriment of his later one.

This is so because there is a perspective to time, as there is to space, and the more immediate needs, like the more immediate objects of vision, often appear bigger and more important than the further ones, even when they are not. The future acquires even less importance because of the fact that tomorrow may never come and thus the sacrifice of today's needs may have been futile. Each individual knows that he will not reach the more distant future, but he also knows that he will probably be living tomorrow. Thus, while most people are inclined to say that today is very important, few people are also inclined to say that tomorrow does not count. Each individual must try to account for the illusion of the perspective of time and to judge if today's satisfaction will be worth tomorrow's want. Thus each individual must judge as to the ideal mixture of present and future satisfaction versus future and present needs so that he may act accordingly. And the individual who sacrifices a lesser immediate satisfaction in favor of a greater, later satisfaction, in spite of appearances, is said to be exercising his *will*.

The concept of will is central to religion and morality and it is important that we should state its simple meaning and examine the misunderstanding which has been prevailing about it.

To will is to exercise a special kind of choice, which is the choice of means rather than the choice of end. This choice often appears wretched, in that it consists in the sacrifice of some satisfaction, and it is only when it is seen that this sacrifice will provide greater satisfaction in the long run that it can be understood that this choice is the recognition of the illusion of the perspective of time and the refusal to be misled by it and that, for this reason, it is the only moral choice that it is possible to make.

But people often fail to grasp this fact and they assume that they are act-ing morally when they exercise their will so as not to satisfy desires, because, somehow, this exercise in itself is absolutely superior to the satisfaction of the desires. This belief is reinforced by those religions which claim that human beings are endowed with "free" will, which makes them capable of choosing evil as well as good, and that, furthermore, they are inclined to desire evil rather than good. This presumption is grounded on the misunder-standing about the meaning of the word *good,* when such is considered to be something which is absolute and objective and which is independent of the individual and his satisfaction. The concept of a will that can desire evil becomes obviously absurd when one understands that a thing is good and desirable exactly because it is satisfactory subjectively and relatively and that the evil is essentially that which is subjectively and relatively unsatisfac-tory and undesirable. Since, for a human being, there is no absolute and objective good independent of himself, of his desires and of his satisfaction, that individual cannot be said to be capable not to desire the satisfaction of his needs, nor can he be said to be capable not to want and to will the means to this satisfaction, which is goodness by definition.

If human beings appear to be capable of choosing evil, it is in the possi-bility of choosing an immediate good which they will later regret when it brings an evil. But an individual, as he made his choice, did not want to choose evil. He wanted the lesser immediate good only because his judg-ment was warped by the illusion of his perspective in time which led him to believe that the lesser good was greater than the greater one.

* * *

But the individual cannot fully appreciate the fact of the perspective of time and he cannot exercise his will to choose the satisfaction of his greater needs to the detriment of his lesser needs unless he has the time to examine and appreciate the alternatives that are available to him. Thus, if a choice must be made quickly, it is more likely than otherwise that the person choosing will opt for the more immediate satisfaction which appears to be greater even though it is not. But, if someone has the time to consider his choice, he may compensate for the illusion of time and choose the more dis-tant satisfaction when he has judged that, in spite of appearances, it is greater than the more immediate satisfaction.

Thus it is to the individual's advantage to consider his needs when they are not yet immediate and when he has the leisure to do so, and then to make resolutions as to how he will act given certain conditions. These reso-lutions are assets which an individual creates for the future. They are made to be stored away and stockpiled, like fuel and food, so that they may be recalled and used when they are needed.

These resolutions are *moral laws* which are necessarily expressed through language and which intend to govern the future behavior of the individual, for his greater good, and in spite of the illusions of the moment.

It is because of these moral laws that an individual, in the future, may perform an act which appears contrary to his end, because of the limited vision of the moment, but which he knows to be valid because he knows the value of his thoughts in the past. Thus an individual can enjoy the benefit of reasoning when he does not have the time for it.

People who make such moral laws, and who abide by them, are said to be acting morally. And it is those individuals who, in time of urgency, allow themselves to distrust their moral laws and who revise them to conform to the appearances of the moment who are said to be acting immorally.

But the fact that an individual has made some moral laws does not mean that he must not make yet new ones or that he must not modify or even abandon those that he has made. In fact he must do all of these things continually.

He must make new moral laws to meet emerging situations and to satisfy newly found needs, which he will acquire until the end of his life.

He must modify existing moral laws for the same reason, which is that his needs change throughout his lifetime, but he must also modify them, because moral laws are statements which are often proved inadequate and in need of perfection.

An individual must perfect his moral laws slowly by a process of trial and error, when he has the leisure to do so and after careful examination to ensure that the new moral law is not worse than the old one. An individual must perfect his moral laws by re-examining the words that he uses in their formulations to ensure that they truly reflect his wants and his desires, and he must continually make improvements by changing these words so that his moral laws are always clearer, and more meaningful, and less ambiguous.

But an individual must often continue to abide by the dictates of his moral laws while he is in the process of reviewing and perfecting them. Their imperfections seldom deprive them of some value and of much value. In fact, if people were to abide only by perfect moral laws, they would seldom abide by *any* moral law and the very thought of moral laws would be of little importance.

But, while an individual must abide by imperfect moral laws, he must abandon those moral laws which have lost all validity. A moral law remains valid as long as it serves the greatest ends of that individual and it ceases to be valid when it no longer serves these ends. Moral laws may or may not state the greatest ends of that individual who they are meant to serve. When they do not state such ends, they should imply them.

However, people often forget such implied ends and continue to comply with their laws even when the ends have ceased to remain valid. It is in these moral laws gone wild that has originated the belief in absolute moral laws, which are purported to exist independently of human purpose. It is to rid himself of them that every individual must always question the purpose of his moral laws to ensure that they are still valid and deserving of respect. And an individual must cease to respect and honor those moral laws which have lost their original purpose and which therefore have ceased to remain valid moral laws.

4

HUMAN PURPOSE

The actions of every conscious being are directed toward one single fundamental purpose, which is to serve the interests of that individual. This statement is true tautologically. It is true because whatever the individual is serving by his action is, by definition, *"the interests"* of that individual. Thus the purpose of every individual is to serve his interests.

In so doing, the individual is at once his own means and his own end. He is his own means because he must act to achieve his end and to serve his interests. He is his own end because it is ultimately his desires and feelings which dictate the needs that he must act to satisfy. This is also true in an obvious and tautological way, and it is self-contradictory to suppose that an individual could be moved by desires and feelings which are not *his* desires and feelings, that he would want to serve the interests of others rather than his own, since this would be to suppose that an effect can be caused by other than its cause.

But every individual cannot satisfy his needs and serve his interests by acting in a vacuum. Every individual must act in an environment and must use that environment to serve those interests. Thus each individual can serve his interests only by exploiting his environment, and he thus wants his environment to be a means and to serve his interests. But what is his environment? To every conscious being, the environment can only be everything that is, except himself. Thus each individual wants to use every possible means to serve his interests. For this reason, it is not enough to say that he does not want to serve the interests of others; it is more exact to add that he wants everything and everyone else to serve his interests. Thus everything and everyone, including every other human being, is a means to the individual.

Thus the value of anything, for an individual, is entirely subjective and relative and lies exclusively in its ability to satisfy his needs. Anything which does not satisfy such needs is not good and has no value. Anything which impedes the satisfaction of his needs without offering the compensating promise of later greater satisfaction is bad and has negative value.

But as each individual endeavors to use everything and everyone that is, as means to serve his interests, he will possibly come in conflict with others. This is so because the means to goodness ₋annot always be good to one without ceasing to be good to someone else, indeed without in fact becoming wretched for the latter. This possibility of conflict is yet greater when one's very person is used as a means by someone else in such a way that one is inhibited from serving one's own interests.

But, while the fact that individuals must serve their interests at the expense of others is clear and evident and while it may be explained logically and rationally, it seems to be contradicted by another undeniable fact, which is that some individuals appear to act as means and to serve the interests of others. Everyone is aware of countless incidences of devotion of individuals to others: to one's child, mate, friend, dog, country, or mankind itself. This devotion can be carried out at the expense of much grief and suffering and even at the risk of one's life. Thus individuals appear in fact to be moved by the feelings of others.

It is possible to explain this fact in part by proposing that an individual must serve others so that others may better serve him. Thus, just as an individual must take care of his tools so that they will not deteriorate and become useless, then, if everyone else is a means to the individual, they are in fact tools which may require to be served so that they may better serve him.

But, while this explanation is valid in many instances, it is not valid all of the time and it is possible to recall numerous incidences where someone or something is being served for no obvious reason.

But if there is no obvious reason, then should we not look for a reason which is not obvious? Should we not ask the question: "Why are you serving another?"? And could the answer not be "I am serving another because I desire to serve another"? Could the answer not invoke the reason without a further reason, the cause without a cause? Is it not possible that the variety of needs, particularly for human beings, is so great that it may include the need to satisfy the needs of someone else?

But when one answers that he is serving another because "he desires to serve another" he is affirming that, in so doing, he is satisfying an ultimate feeling and as such he is also affirming that the other is merely a means to the satisfaction of this feeling. And this feeling is one's own feeling and not another's. Thus one does not satisfy another's feeling except indirectly through one's own feeling. Thus the individual who serves another or something else merely appears to be a means while he is not. And it is those who appear to be the ends that are in fact the means.

And it is this explanation which alone can rescue the humanist principle from appearing to contradict the facts. But it is not only the humanist principle which is explained; it is also the facts about human nature and purpose which would themselves otherwise be self-contradictory.

But is this explanation adequate to satisfy all possible cases? Is it possible to acknowledge that, although many individuals may serve their own interests while appearing to serve the interests of others, there are still incidences of individuals who genuinely serve the interests of others while not serving their own, who serve the wants of others when these wants are contrary to their own wants and in spite of their own feelings and desires?

Humanism proposes that this may be acknowledged and explained. And the explanation is that which is applicable to all anti-humanism. Thus all anti-humanism is possible because of the nature of human language, which allows human beings to speak in meaningless and self-contradictory terms and then to act in accordance with their speech. It is possible because individuals have failed to use their rational faculty and have failed to recognize that goodness is only meaningful when it is considered to be relative and subjective and they have accepted without question that there is an absolute goodness whereby it is better for one to satisfy the feelings and desires of others rather than one's own. They have failed to recognize that it is self-contradictory to suppose that it is better for oneself to do what is not good for oneself, that it is better for oneself to do what is good for others rather than oneself, that one must choose to satisfy the wants of others rather than one's own wants. These individuals have come to act as if they were not themselves but someone else. They have lost their own identity. They are living self-contradictions.

They have become so because they have failed to think; they have failed to seek a relationship of cause and effect about themselves and their actions; they have failed to ask the fundamental moral question. They have failed to ask: "Why am I serving another; am I satisfying a need which is ultimately dictated by a feeling; in other words, *do I have a reason to do so*?"

Once someone has asked this question he has also asked: "Should I act as I do?" Once someone has asked this question he has awakened to reason. If he should answer yes to his question, then he can recognize that this reason can only be himself and that he is not truly serving another; while if he should answer no, then he will recognize that he is living in contradiction to his nature, that the rational individual must be his own purpose and serve his interests, and he will be moved to change his ways and to act in accordance with his reason.

* * *

It is impossible to consider human purpose without addressing the principle of many theist religions which claim that all things, including every living being and particularly human beings, were created by God to serve the divine purpose and that therefore the purpose of mankind, by virtue of its very existence, is undeniably to serve God. It is also a tenet of these religions that, while everything, including nonhuman living beings, will have no choice but to perform their duty and to serve God, human beings are capable of refusing to fulfill their appointed duty.

It is tempting to challenge this belief by questioning the existence of God. But such a challenge would be meaningless exactly because the word "God" by itself is meaningless. The word "God" can only become meaningful if the nature of God is explained. Then it is only when we have considered what sort of a God would create human beings for His purpose that we may consider if His existence is reasonable. But the fact that we could challenge the existence of that particular God does not mean that we have challenged the existence of any and every possible God.

Those who believe in a God-Creator often make the extraordinary claim that such a God has no needs because He is perfect. This claim is extraordinary on two counts. First, it is that the absence of needs is not perfection because it is the existence of needs, which are capable of being satisfied, which makes the existence of conscious beings worthwhile.

The second and even more extraordinary count is that the absence of needs in a God-Creator should deny the existence of mankind and indeed of the world. If such a God is perfect and without needs, why would He create mankind and the world? If there is such a God, then mankind and the world do not exist. And the existence of mankind and the world is a proof that such a God does not exist!

Then, obviously, the only kind of God that could have created mankind and the world would have to be a God with needs, a God like man and with a need for the services of mankind.

And how could human beings satisfy the needs of such a God? How have they been expected to satisfy these needs? What do those religions that proclaim such a God usually say about the needs of their God? What do they teach that human beings should do except humiliate themselves and bow to the ground to acknowledge the dominance of God and to offer sacrifices, to submit to suffering, and to inflict it upon others to please and appease Him?

But why would God need human submission and suffering? These do not serve any obvious purpose. Why would anyone have such needs? Why do human beings themselves have such needs? But we know, in most cases, why human beings have such needs: it is for reasons which are not obvious; it is for the reasons beyond moral reasons; it is for meta-moral reasons. It is for reasons which are buried in the genetic heritage and the past conditioning of the individual; and we are now discovering that human beings tend to be more cruel and abusive of others when they have suffered traumatic experiences in their younger years. They then feel inferior and threatened and they need and seek by their actions to be reassured of their worth and security. But God has no genetic heritage and has had no traumatic experiences. How then can we explain God's need of cruelty? What are His metamoral reasons?

But, then, what about human beings under such a God? The fact is that human beings, for the most part, have no inclination to serve and to suffer. Even individuals who have been brought up in theocentric societies and who have had a belief in God pounded into their heads from birth rebel against God. Those people would not think of questioning, and would think even less of denying the existence of God, and of the kind of God that demands submission and suffering; and yet they resist, with all their might and at the cost of heart-rending remorses, the obligation they feel they have to serve Him. Why would God create such a being and set him in such an insoluble and intolerable situation of conflict and unhappiness?

If God wanted to be attended by subservient and suffering human beings, why did he not create them with a desire to serve Him in this manner? Why did He not create them with the faithful souls of dogs and with masochistic cravings? Why did God create human beings that do not all have a desire to serve Him.

The explanation which is most commonly advanced is that there is a reciprocity of purpose between God and human beings whereby human beings cannot satisfy their greatest ultimate need until they have accepted to submit to God's whims. But if this were true, why is it possible that so many individuals do not feel this need?

To answer this objection, it has been proposed that human beings would have that need if they "experienced" God and that it is only because of the lack of an immediate knowledge of God that they refuse to enter into the desired relationship with Him. But, if this need may only develop because of a personal acquaintance with God, why does God not make Himself as available as possible so that there is no question as to His existence and as to His value to human beings, rather than allow so many individuals to be confused about their greatest ultimate need? Why must God play a game of hide-and-seek, except to satisfy His own cruel need of entertainment?

But then God is not satisfied to enjoy frustrating His creatures by denying them adequate knowledge of His existence, His power, and His goodness, but He will punish those who lack this adequate knowledge and who refuse to serve what they have concluded does not exist. He will punish rather than admire those who are acting rationally!

But while it is possible to question the existence of such a God, we must recognize that His existence is not a logical impossibility, that the idea of such a God is not self-contradictory, and that mankind may truly be afflicted by a nightmarish fate at the hands of such a God.

But whether such a God exists or not is not the most important fact that concerns humanism and humanist morality. This is true because the existence of such a God would not challenge humanism and its principle. Thus whatever God may be, if there is a God, and whatever His nature and purpose may be, the humanist principle that every human being, like every conscious being, is his own purpose remains wholly true.

Thus it is not sufficient that God exists and that He has created human beings for his purpose to make it so that human purpose is God. This is true by virtue of the fact that human beings are conscious beings and that a conscious being is his own purpose. This is true whether a human being is serving God because of a compulsive desire to serve Him or because of a desire to avoid God's punishment. It is true whether a human being has the faithful soul of a dog or is a coldly calculating cajoler.

Thus, even if God has created human beings for His purpose, the purpose of each human being would not be God for that individual. The purpose of that individual would be God only from God's point of view. In fact, inasmuch as that individual is concerned, God is part of the environment and, as such, the purpose of God Himself is that individual's! Thus the purpose of that individual could only have the appearance of being God, and this would occur if this individual chooses to serve his interests indirectly by serving the interests of God directly. Thus the ultimate purpose of every individual can only be himself whether God exists or not.

* * *

But God has a competitor. It is *Nature*. Thus, there is a prevalent belief that all living beings have a "natural purpose" which exists independently of their desires and feelings and which may be discovered by observing Nature. Thus this purpose is deemed to be manifest and one has only to look at reality to see the clear evidence of its existence.

Thus it may be proposed that deer exist for the purpose of feeding wolves and that the denial of God, as the consciousness Who has created this purpose, would merely reinforce the fact that purpose exists in Nature independently of a mind.

It is also proposed that sexual functions exist for the manifest purpose of reproduction and that the practice of birth control is contrary to the natural purpose of sexuality.

When one seeks purpose in Nature, one has failed to recognize that the purpose of nonconscious beings is not in the being itself but that all purpose is the product of a rational function and that it can only exist in the mind of a conscious being where it is a reflection of his desires and his feelings. Where there is no conscious being there is no purpose. Nature is not a conscious being. Nature is reality, which is everything that can be experienced. Conscious beings are part of Nature, but Nature itself is not a conscious being. Nature cannot "want" or "desire," and it is to speak metaphorically, and therefore meaninglessly, to suppose that it can. Thus, there is no manifest purpose to be found in Nature.

The purpose of anything may only be found in the thing itself if that thing is a conscious being, and then its purpose cannot be separated from its own reason, desires, and feelings. Thus consciousness is the source of purpose and the being who has consciousness will generate its own purpose. And each individual conscious being will generate its purpose independently of and often in opposition to the other individuals.

Thus deer do not exist to feed wolves but they happen to feed wolves because they exist. It is not the purpose of Nature that wolves should eat deer but it is the purpose of wolves to eat deer just as it is the purpose of deer not to be eaten by wolves.

What is true of deer and wolves is all the truer of human beings who are endowed of more consciousness than deer and wolves. Thus human beings have no reason to look at Nature to discover the purpose of anything so that they may conform themselves to what it seems to say about itself, but they must look at their own desires and feelings where they will see self-evident reasons to compel Nature to serve their purpose.

Thus, human beings may want to act sexually or not as they want to act in any other way: to satisfy their needs as dictated by their desires and feelings. Thus, each individual must decide for himself whether or not he will act sexually, how he will act and whether or not reproduction will have anything to do with it.

When an individual wants to act sexually while not desiring to reproduce, then sexuality is an ultimate end, and reproduction, if it should occur, is merely a by-product, and possibly an undesirable by-product. In the latter case, it is only inasmuch as the by-product is unavoidable that it will be tolerated.

When, on the other hand, an individual truly wants or desires to reproduce, then sexuality becomes merely a means to this end for this individual.

Thus, as each individual decides, he must consider his feelings and desires and he has no reason to consider the choice of others nor the apparent dictates of Nature. Thus, every conscious being is his own purpose and neither God, nor Nature, nor anything or anyone else can stand as his purpose.

PART THREE

THE HUMANIST MINISTRY

5

THE THEORY

If a religion is a system of beliefs about human nature and purpose, then the goal of those who support a given religion is to promote its beliefs and to convince others to adopt them.

But, while this goal applies to every religion, it applies more particularly to nonhumanism than to humanism. This is so because humanism is the religion that exists by default. If there were no anti-humanism, one could be a humanist without being aware that it is possible to be otherwise.

Thus, once humanism has proposed that human nature is to seek the good and that each conscious being has no other purpose but himself, and after it has explained that the failure of human beings to recognize their true nature and purpose is imputable to misuses and abuses of language, humanism has achieved its goal, because it has presented the essential of its belief. It may now invite others to reconsider their own beliefs in a logical and meaningful way to ensure that they are not living in contradiction to their nature and purpose. And a humanist may be willing to help an individual sort out his beliefs, if he is invited to do so, but he does not seek this role. He will not attempt to impose himself upon others because he would then be defeating his own purpose.

This is true because the individual cannot be helped until he recognizes that he needs this help and until he is willing to seek and accept it. Thus, by harassing an individual who does not feel this need and who wants to be left alone, one cannot help that individual but one may only add to the misfortune that he must endure.

Thus, as long as the individual remains silent about his nature and purpose, then whatever he may be doing does not give the humanist cause to

47

believe that such an individual is acting contrary to his nature and purpose. The humanist must assume that the individual is happy in his condition and he must respect his apparent desire to be left alone.

But the individual is not usually left alone to himself; he is constantly solicited to act in one way or another by the nonhumanist religions. And it is because of this presence of nonhumanist religions, as an active force in society, always soliciting the people to behave in one way or another, that humanism acquires a further role in society, beyond that of stating its principle.

This role is to represent the individual who is being solicited by the non-humanists and to carry out the kind of dialogue with the nonhumanists that this individual is either incapable of or unwilling to carry out for himself.

Inasmuch as a nonhumanist religion is more properly anti-humanist and affirms that a human being is not his own purpose and must not seek what is good for him, the humanist must contradict anti-humanism and affirm its own principle as self-evident and tautological, while affirming that the anti-humanist principle is self-contradictory and meaningless.

Inasmuch as a nonhumanist religion is such without being anti-humanist, the humanist must question the principle which underlies this religion when it solicits others to act in one way or another. It must ask why an individual should act in such a way.

The individual, when he is solicited, and the humanist, when he acts as the agent of that individual, are justified to pose this question, because any-one who affirms that another ought to act in one way or another should give a reason why one ought to do so. This is true of anyone in any society, because anyone who would tell anyone else what he ought to do, without telling him why he ought to do so, would be speaking meaninglessly and would deserve to be ignored.

And, when a nonhumanist is asked to provide a reason, he cannot be allowed to provide *any* kind of reason: the only acceptable reason must be one which is logical and meaningful.

Thus, once he has been given a reason, the humanist must analyze this reason to ensure that it is logical and meaningful and to point out when and why it fails to be so. If he should point out that the reason is illogical or meaningless, the humanist has also pointed out that the reason given is not truly a reason, in which case the humanist is justified to repeat his question and to inquire again as to this reason.

Ultimately, there is only one reason that one should want to do some-thing. And it is that *his* action serves *his* interests and produces the good to satisfy *his* needs as dictated by *his* feelings and desires. Any other reason is invalid and meaningless.

Then again, ultimately, there is only one individual who can say if the reason is valid and meaningful. It is the individual whose needs must be sat-isfied. This is so because he is the only one who really knows *his* feelings and desires. Thus the reason must not be one that satisfies the religious minister's feelings and desires but one that satisfies the feelings and desires of the individual who is being solicited.

Thus the nonhumanist minister must not be allowed to speak as if his own feelings and desires are the only possible feelings and desires, but he must be asked to consider that others may have different characters and personalities and, thus, that they may have different feelings and desires. The nonhumanist minister must be told that he can have the feelings and desires that he wants but that he must accept that others may also enjoy the same privilege.

Thus the humanist minister must not allow the nonhumanist minister to subject the people to arrogant and self-righteous predication. He must not allow the nonhumanist to dictate to the people, but he must insist that the nonhumanist be polite and patient in trying to convince them that *his* beliefs are logical and meaningful and in accordance with *their* feelings and desires. The humanist minister must also insist that the nonhumanist minister accept graciously that some or all of the people remain unconvinced or uninterested, in spite of all his efforts, and that he respects their desire to be left alone.

The humanist minister must teach the people how to reprove and condemn and ignore any preacher who speaks *at them* rather than *with them,* who pounds pulpits and points fingers, who does not invite dialogue as an equal to equals, who does not consider and respect their feelings and desires, and who insists on soliciting them without their permission and after having been asked to desist.

But the nonhumanist minister is not always only satisfied to try to convince others to do as he would have them do, and he is often led to compel them to do so! He will want to compel them by threatening them with deprivation, ostracism, and even aggression.

In such a situation, it is no longer the reasons that others might have to do as the nonhumanist wishes that matter, but it is the reasons of the nonhumanist himself that become of interest to all concerned.

This is so because the nonhumanist minister is no longer acting entirely as a religious minister whose primary purpose is to convince others to act in accordance with their nature and purpose, but he is also acting as a politician, whose own needs must be satisfied by the actions of others.

And these others cannot be free from the nonhumanist minister simply by ignoring him. They cannot ignore the threat of aggression, ostracism, or deprivation and they must act to free themselves from this threat. They may only do so by considering the interests of the individual who is threatening them rather than their own interests and by attempting to convince such an individual that the latter's interests are not truly served by compelling them.

Thus, whenever anyone is threatening to use his power and prerogatives to compel others, this individual has lost his status of religious minister and it is others, including his victims, who are now acting in this role. It is for this reason that this individual must not be allowed to talk in terms of his victims' interests, but only in terms of his own. And it is as an agent of the victims that the humanist may intervene and try to dissuade this individual from his intentions.

And, as we have seen, the humanist, or the victims, may only try to dissuade the tormentor by showing him that he is not serving his interests by compelling others. To do so, one must first inquire from the tormentor to establish if he wishes to compel others as a means or otherwise as an end and by gearing one's arguments to the explanation given.

Thus, if the tormentor states that he is compelling others as a means, one may attempt to dissuade him by showing him that his compelling action will not produce the desired end and therefore that it is not a true means and that it should be abandoned.

If, on the other hand, the tormentor states that he is compelling others as an end, and that the compelling action itself satisfies a desire, then one may only attempt to dissuade him by showing him that his actions are in conflict with a greater end to which it should be sacrificed.

But, if the humanist or the victims fail in both approaches, and if they must then admit that it is impossible to show that the action is not a valid means, or that the action is in conflict with a greater end, then the humanist and the victims must recognize that the tormentor and his intended victims are involved in a conflict of interests which is primarily a political matter rather than a religious matter and which requires a political solution rather than a religious solution.

*   *   *

Since the humanist's role is not to affirm his beliefs but to question the nonhumanist's beliefs, then their respective ministries should also be very different.

Thus, while the nonhumanist minister will be primarily concerned with speaking to the people and dictating what they should do, the humanist will be primarily concerned with speaking to the nonhumanist minister.

The humanist is not primarily interested in speaking to the people except to reassure them when they are being solicited by the nonhumanist and to convince them that they must not feel guilty because they do not wish to comply with the nonhumanist's admonitions. The humanist must explain to them that it is not they who must justify their actions to the religious minister but that it is the religious minister who must justify his beliefs to them and that they are under no obligation to even speak or listen to a religious minister. The humanist must also demonstrate how he will speak to the nonhumanist, and how they can do as he does, if they wish — how they can question the nonhumanist about the latter's beliefs and how they can detect and demonstrate where the nonhumanist is speaking in self-contradictory and meaningless terms, when he does so.

Because of their different approaches, the humanist is at once justified to pose questions to the nonhumanist and to refuse to answer the latter's questions. But the fact that the humanist is justified to pose questions does not mean that he should do so.

The humanist must remember that his first purpose is to promote humanism. And how better to promote humanism than to convince the nonhumanist himself?

But, if the humanist is to convince the nonhumanist, he must try to speak to him in a conciliatory fashion and try to avoid any approach which may be antagonistic. And it is the humanist question itself which may be antagonistic!

This is so because questions are often naturally antagonistic. The only questions which are not antagonistic are those which are posed for the exclusive and indisputable purpose of seeking information. But the humanist questions cannot be posed for this exclusive purpose because everyone knows that they are also posed to show nonhumanist beliefs to be defective.

But then how is the humanist to deal with the nonhumanists if he is to try to avoid posing questions?

This may be done if the humanist does not frame his questions as questions, but rather as declarative statements or as series of declarative statements. And these statements could stand in lieu of questions if they reflect one's failure to understand what the other has expressed so as to elicit an explanation or a recognition that there is truly a problem, without explicitly demanding such explanation or recognition.

Thus, the humanist must deal with the nonhumanist by means of a dialogue which is composed mainly of declarative statements and where a question would only be allowed when there is a clear purpose to seek some particular item of information rather than to challenge a belief.

And, if the latter condition must be respected, then it is the individual who must answer the question who remains the sole judge of whether such a purpose is clear. Thus this individual may inquire as to the purpose of the question and, if he is dissatisfied with the explanation, he may, without prejudice, refuse to answer this question as well as request that his interlocutor frame his question in a declarative manner.

This approach should be acceptable to the nonhumanist because it is no longer implying that the nonhumanist beliefs are invalid but only that they are misunderstood and that they require to be explained. It places the humanist and the nonhumanist on the same footing; while they are still playing different roles, they may now both claim to have a common goal, which is to seek a mutual understanding about the nonhumanist beliefs.

In professing to seek a mutual understanding the participants to the dialogue have avoided appearing to be pitted against personal enemies; they have both agreed to cooperate to overcome their own intellectual shortcomings, and their method consists in addressing these shortcomings rather than confronting each other.

If the humanist is to be honest in this approach, he must make it as easy as possible for his interlocutor to abandon his beliefs. He must never claim a victory over his interlocutor, but he must state that it is to the credit of his interlocutor that the latter is discovering new beliefs.

Furthermore, the humanist must not consider that he is immune to the acquisition of new beliefs and he must be ready to acknowledge, as graciously as possible, when his interlocutor is speaking logically and meaningfully and imparting some worthwhile knowledge.

* * *

The humanist is not interested in participating in a dialogue that has no purpose, that drifts aimlessly and inconclusively, and that drags on forever. The humanist has a clear direction in mind, he knows where he wants the dialogue to lead, and he wants to participate in the dialogue in ways that will set it and keep it on its course and achieve its purpose, which is to reach a mutual understanding with his interlocutor about the latter's beliefs.

This participation will consist in the kind of responses the humanist will contribute to the dialogue that he must keep up with the nonhumanist. His responses must have the single-mindedness and the sobriety that can only discourage diversion. Thus the humanist responses must be renowned for two essential qualities: *unity of purpose* and *brevity*.

Thus, to ensure that the dialogue remains on course and to prevent diversions, the humanist's response should address only one point and it must address this point as briefly as possible. It does not matter how many points are addressed by the nonhumanist's response or how elaborate the response may be. If necessary, the humanist's response must contrast sharply with his interlocutor's: in time, the effectiveness of his approach will be evident.

Thus, as he begins to participate in a dialogue, the humanist must first select his point by analyzing his prospective interlocutor's statement of beliefs and by identifying the most important point in it. It is this point that the humanist should select to address until it is resolved.

The necessity of selecting the most important point cannot be overemphasized. If the humanist should happen to select a secondary, marginal, or subordinate point, he will have condemned the dialogue to drift aimlessly.

It must be stressed that the point that the humanist must select must be a part of his interlocutor's statement of beliefs and not a part of his own. This approach follows necessarily from the very different and particular roles of the humanist and the nonhumanist in the dialogue.

This approach is necessary for another important reason: it is to ensure that the dialogue remains a dialogue. The dialogue cannot remain a dialogue if neither of the participants is listening to the other and responding to what the other is saying. Such an exchange would be a twin soliloquy rather than a dialogue. Of course the humanist cannot prevent his interlocutor from indulging in a soliloquy, but he can avoid doing so himself. And because of his particular role, his efforts will be sufficient to salvage the character of the dialogue, whatever his interlocutor may do. Thus the humanist may be very attentive to his interlocutor: he must be very careful to respond to what he says.

Thus each response of the humanist, while it addresses the most important point of the dialogue as he sees it, must respond directly to his interlocutor's previous response. Again, the humanist must select the most important point in that response, which will usually be directly related to the most important point of the dialogue, and he must address this point alone.

It is only when the most important point of the dialogue has been resolved that the humanist may undertake to address the second most important point, if it is still relevant.

Of course, as the dialogue progresses, it is quite possible that a new point will emerge which is obviously more important than the original one: in such a case, the humanist should then abandon the original point, for the time being, and consider this new one exclusively, until it is resolved, before returning to the original point.

The fact that the humanist must respond to his interlocutor and address the latter's beliefs rather than his own does not mean that the humanist leaves the initiative to his interlocutor. To the contrary, if the humanist must steer the dialogue toward the desired goal, he must retain the initiative. He does so by choosing the point to be considered, as we have seen. But he must also do so in relation to the meaning of the words that are used by his interlocutor.

Thus, in the process of addressing the most important point, the humanist must be particularly attentive to the meanings of the words. This is so because the meaning of a statement is always dependent upon the meanings of the words within it, so that the self-contradiction and meaninglessness of a statement can often be traced to such meanings. Thus it is important that the meanings of the words used in statements, and particularly in the nonhumanist statements, be clarified.

And, in the process of seeking such a clarification, the humanist must not ask his interlocutor to "define his terms." This negative approach would be useless because the nonhumanist is often confused as to the meanings of the words that he uses and his definitions would only set the dialogue adrift into more self-contradictions and meaninglessness. Thus it is by defining the words himself that the humanist may direct and redirect the course of the dialogue, and this is why it is so important that he retain this function for himself.

It is for this reason that the humanist must always speak as if he knows the meanings of the words that are used. If he does not, he must develop his own meanings by analyzing the common usages of the words and by consulting dictionaries and other sources of reference.

The humanist must accept the popular definitions, as revealed by the common usages or the dictionaries, unless such definitions are themselves self-contradictory, meaningless, or ambiguous, in which case the humanist must point out this difficulty and propose his own definitions that would remove this difficulty. In extreme cases, he may have to propose that a word is inherently meaningless and that it should not be used.

As he seeks a definition, the humanist must particularly seek to highlight the subjective and relative meanings of many words which can cause so much ambiguity when they are overlooked. He must also call attention to whatever words are used metaphorically and which can only lead to absurdity.

In summary, in participating in a dialogue with the nonhumanist, the humanist should usually respond to his interlocutor by first defining the words as he understands them so as to explain how the interlocutor appears to have been led to self-contradictions and meaninglessness because he was not aware of the true meanings of the words that he used, and particularly the true relative and subjective meanings of words which he was using in an absolute and objective sense.

* * *

But, in spite of his best intentions, the humanist cannot succeed in achieving a mutual understanding with his interlocutor unless the latter is willing to contribute, as well as being intellectually capable of contributing, to the dialogue in ways that will serve its purpose: unless he is honest as well as competent. And the humanist is no more interested in participating in a dialogue that cannot serve its purpose than to one that has no purpose.

It is easy to understand that individuals may be incompetent. But why would individuals be dishonest? Why would one agree to participate in a dialogue and yet be unwilling to serve its purpose? This is only possible because individuals fail to separate their beliefs from themselves and, thus, they feel personally threatened when their beliefs are challenged. For this reason, they consider their interlocutors as enemies to be defeated, and they consider the dialogue as merely another battlefield.

These individuals use words as weapons rather than as means of communication. They participate in the dialogue to inflict harm upon their adversaries and have no intention of reaching a mutual understanding with them. As such, they are misusing words and dialogue, and their participation is dishonest. Thus, by honesty, the humanist means the attitude of an individual toward his interlocutor and toward the dialogue.

The humanist engages in the dialogue with only one assumption and one purpose. The assumption is that he and his interlocutor have a common interest to search for a mutual understanding, and the purpose is to do everything possible to reach this understanding. And the humanist expects his interlocutor to share the same assumption and purpose.

The humanist will always be careful never to identify or even appear to identify his own person or that of his interlocutor with his respective belief. And he will expect that his interlocutor will have the same care so as not to jeopardize the conduct and the goal of the dialogue.

This is why the humanist will not involve, nor appear to involve, the person of his interlocutor in any way or form, nor will he allow his own person to be involved or appear to be involved. He will insist that the participants discuss the subject of the dialogue, while leaving out the persons of the participants. He will insist that the participants do not involve one another indirectly by showing distrust of one another, by implying accusations of deceit and ulterior motives, but that they accept at face value what each other says about his experiences and his intentions. He will insist that the participants be scrupulously and demonstratively polite, considerate, and conciliatory toward one another.

He will grant that each participant must be free to consider any attempt to involve his person in any way or form as an attempt to identify the person and the beliefs.

The humanist will respond to any such attempt by stating categorically that he refuses to allow his person to be involved, just as he will not allow himself to involve the persons of others. He will emphasize his response by abandoning any other consideration and by making this statement constitute the whole of his response. If his interlocutor should persist in his objectionable approach, the humanist should explain why this approach is inherently dishonest and why he must terminate the dialogue if it is continued.

(It is important to point out that it is only in purely religious dialogues that the person of the interlocutor must not be discussed. Inasmuch as the dialogue has a political flavor, as is the case when one is not satisfied to convince others to act in one way or another but wishes to compel them to do so, then the person of tormentor must unavoidably be discussed in his intentions, if he is to be dissuaded from compelling others.)

But honesty alone cannot guarantee a successful dialogue: there is also the problem of competence. If the dialogue is to succeed, the participants must also be competent. They must have the ability and the will, given enough time, to think logically and meaningfully. This is the ability to recognize explicit self-contradictions for what they are and the desire to avoid them. It is also the ability to recognize that tautologies are worthless and should also be avoided except to contradict self-contradictions. Each individual is variously endowed with this ability and some individuals are so seriously deprived of it that meaningful dialogue with them is very difficult.

But the competence of individuals may be improved or worsened by the manner in which the dialogue is conducted. It is obvious that the performance of an individual can only be improved if he has an opportunity to recall and examine what he and his interlocutor have said in the past. It is also obvious that the performance of this individual will be further improved if he has the time to think about his response thoroughly before expressing it.

These facts lead to the conclusion that the form of the dialogue, where the competence and performance of the participants would be enhanced and which would lead to a better mutual understanding, would be the written form.

It is obvious that the written dialogue has the advantage that it grants, to the participants, greater opportunities to analyze what has been said, to detect the more subtle misuses and abuses of language, to work and rework one's response to ensure that it is briefer, more precise, and more effective, and that it avoids the pitfalls related to the use of language. The written dialogue does not only serve to increase the competence of the participants, but it invites to honesty by removing the opportunity to use one's strong personality to intimidate one's interlocutor and by reducing, for this interlocutor, the feeling of being challenged in his person and the temptation of defending himself by involving in turn the person of his interlocutor, thereby sabotaging the conduct of the dialogue.

Of course the written dialogue is a much slower process, but the humanist is not primarily concerned with speed but with reaching a mutual understanding, which requires time and thought rather than improvisation and impulsiveness. This is why the humanist will always prefer the written dialogue; and he will be particularly wary when he is compelled, by circumstances, to engage in an oral dialogue, and he must then express his qualms very clearly to his interlocutor.

But, whatever form the humanist dialogue may take, it must not take on the aspect of a *debate*! The latter is merely a game of histrionics whose obvious purpose is to exhibit one's personality and intellectual superiority and to show off one's wits rather than to help others overcome their shortcomings. It is significant that the preferred form of the debate is oral.

Debates, by their very nature, can only lead to misunderstanding rather than mutual understanding. In a debate, the participants are intentionally opposed on a point and each is personally identified to his adopted cause, although he is not necessarily expected to believe in it. The participants in a debate are expected to win and to lose, not by helping to resolve the question to everyone's satisfaction by resolving self-contradictions and meaninglessness without appearing to do so, but rather by embarrassing their opponents, by tricking them into uttering self-contradictory and meaningless statements or even by accusing them of uttering such statements when it is not true. The participants to a debate cannot be concerned with the subject being discussed, which is not important, but must be concerned with each other's person: they must score points by being witty at each other's expense, and the outcome is more mirth than enlightenment.

In the context of a dialogue about religion, the humanist must always consider all rhetorical flights, as are indulged in, in debates, as mere misuses and abuses of language that are impeding the proper progress of the dialogue, and he must humorlessly denounce them for what they are, even at the risk of appearing stupid.

And, if ever the humanist is tempted to participate in a debate, he should warn all concerned that he cannot and does not do so in his capacity as a humanist.

6

THE PRACTICE

Of all the causes in which the humanist may be involved, there are few that can match the abortion debate in its potential to illustrate the humanist faith and method and that offer to the humanist such an ideal opportunity to perform in his role as a humanist. This is so because there have been few causes that have offered such occasions to misuse and abuse language and where the occasions have been seized more earnestly. There have also been few causes in our modern society where the misuses and abuses of language have been at the root of so much self-inflicted and unnecessary misery and suffering and where the contribution of humanism has been more sorely needed.

Yet, in spite of the fact that abortion is probably the most widely and fiercely discussed and debated moral question in our society today, the humanist is virtually excluded from all participation. It is true that some who claim to be humanists are participating in the debate, but, in so doing, they are seldom in the forefront and never participating in a truly distinct role. They are merely joining those nonhumanists who do not oppose abortion, and they merely adopt and repeat their arguments.

And how is the debate going? It is going nowhere! The debate is an exercise in futility and frustration, where the opponents are condemned to repeat the same arguments over and over again without convincing or hoping to convince each other. They are no longer listening to each other; they only pretend to talk to each other while they are in fact talking to third parties, who are the uncommitted people whom they want to convert to their cause and the politicians whom they want to intimidate in favor of their cause.

And what are their arguments: the arguments of the nonhumanists who oppose abortion and the arguments of those who would allow abortion?

Among those who oppose abortion, there are a number who will base their stand on a theological ground and claim that human life was created by God and that only God has the right to take it away. Of course these people cannot expect others to share their viewpoint about abortion unless others also share their belief in God and in their particular kind of God. As a consequence, these individuals cannot defend their position by speaking of abortion as much as by speaking of God and trying to prove His existence and nature.

A large number of those who oppose abortion and would forbid it are not pleased by this limitation. This is particularly true in pluralistic societies where no one wants to be accused of imposing his religion upon others. To avoid this accusation, these people have proposed that opposition to abortion does not require a belief in God and of a special God but rather a belief in a natural law which grants to every human being a natural right to life and forbids his killing except to defend one's own life. Accordingly, these people claim that their stand is not based on a religious belief but on reason, and therefore they expect that everyone should share that stand.

All of those who oppose abortion, whether for theological reasons or not, propose that human life has an inherent sacredness and that the unborn child has been human since conception. They will present medical evidence to support this fact and they will conclude that all abortions are merely infanticides and that, as such, an abortion is a murder and a crime.

It is for this reason that those who oppose abortion are not satisfied to avoid abortion for themselves, nor are they satisfied to convince others that they should avoid it, but feel justified to prevent others from performing or undergoing abortion and to punish those that do.

Those who oppose abortion often claim that, indirectly, they are serving their own interests by preventing abortion. Thus they claim that abortion will cheapen the value of human life, that it will lead from infanticide to euthanasia and even to compulsory euthanasia and that eventually no one's life will be safe. Thus they often put forth the idea that the right to life is the basis of all other rights and that the latter cannot exist without the former. They have proposed that this right cannot be granted to one without being granted to all, including the unborn, and that, for this reason, the protection of the law, as it applies to children, should also apply to the unborn.

Those who oppose abortion will invoke a number of secondary reasons to support their stand, such as the propositions that women seek abortions for "selfish and frivolous reasons," that the unborn should not be killed "because he is innocent," that the medical practitioners are forbidden by the very terms of their professional oath to perform abortion, that the medical profession and facilities should not perform or be used to perform abortions since "pregnancy is neither a disease nor an injury," and that the unborn child is not only the child of his mother but also of his father and that, for this reason, the latter should have a say in the matter.

And now what are the arguments of those who do not oppose abortion?

The principal claim of these people is that women have a right to safe abortions and that abortions are denied to women by a male-dominated society that wishes to oppress women, and in particular poor women. They also claim that unwanted children should not be allowed to be born since they will be made to suffer for their intrusion into the lives of those who do not want them.

They further usually claim that the unborn is not a human being. And some suggest that a newborn should not be immediately considered as a human being by the laws of the state so that, upon birth, deformed and deficient children may be killed.

Those who do not oppose abortion often claim that they do not like abortion but that it is a necessary evil. They propose that the number of abortions would be reduced if better methods of birth control were available to the people, and that abortions should not be used as a method of birth control.

*   *   *

It may not be self-evident to everyone how the opposing arguments of the abortion debate are afflicted by self-contradictions and meaninglessness, how words with relative and subjective meanings are given absolute and objective meanings, and how words are lent meanings which do not belong to them. It may not be self-evident to everyone how these misuses and abuses of language are the real cause of the misunderstanding and ill feelings between those who are opposed on the abortion question, but this fact must be very evident to the humanist.

It is because of this lucidity that the humanist may particularly join in the debate and make it into a true dialogue. He may do so because he may particularly speak with effectiveness to both sides and lead them to an understanding of the problem that truly confronts them and to a fruitful resolution of their differences.

To achieve this end, the humanist must first make the opponents aware that they are seeking a political solution to a problem which is essentially moral in nature and which can only allow of an intellectual solution. The humanist must then engage in the debate with the promise that he can help them develop this intellectual solution and lead them to a mutual understanding that will remove the temptation of considering a political solution.

The humanist must approach the abortion problem as he does every other moral problem, by proposing the principle that it is the individual who claim that others must act in one way or another who must state why others must do so. This approach will necessarily dictate the humanist role in the dialogue as well as the roles of all the other participants.

In line with this approach, the humanist must point out that abortion should not be allowed because there are reasons to allow it, but because there are no reasons to forbid it. Thus it is useless to offer arguments in favor of abortion and the only reasonable arguments are those against abortion. Thus it is those who oppose abortion who must give reasons for their stand and it is the role of those who would allow abortion to judge of these reasons. And these roles cannot be reversed.

This is why those who would allow abortion must particularly listen to their opponents and respond to them in terms of the latter's arguments and that they should not expect that it is their interlocutors who should respond to them. It is partly in attempting to play the same aggressive role as their opponents, rather than the complementary defensive role, better suited to their position on the abortion question, that those who do not oppose abortion have created the stalemate that afflicts the abortion debate. Thus they must share a larger part of the blame for the failure of the debate.

If the humanist is to reconcile the opponents, then he must approach the abortion question without arguments of his own. Thus he must listen to the others' arguments before he may develop his own and before he may respond to them: and he must respond to them *in their terms*.

This explains why the humanist must approach the abortion question claiming neutrality. He does not claim to be in favor of abortion, but rather he claims that "he cannot see a reason to oppose it." The humanist does not claim that such a reason does not exist but only that he does not know of such a reason. Accordingly, his approach is essentially negative.

Since the humanist does not see a reason to oppose abortion, he has very little to say to—or to hear from—those who do not oppose abortion. All that he can do is to listen to them as they speak to their opponents and to establish the cause of their ineffectiveness. He will see that in their eagerness to respond they do not think. As a result, they are the victims of the same misuses and abuses of language as their opponents and they often unwittingly agree with their opponents exactly where they should not and the humanist must show them that it is for this reason that they weaken their case: rather than convince their opponents to change their point of view, they reinforce that point of view.

Thus it is with those who oppose abortion that the humanist must deal and, in so doing, he must show those who would allow abortion how they should do as he does.

The humanist undertakes to discuss abortion by stating that he has no reasons to oppose abortion and, in so doing, he is asking those who oppose abortion to give him reasons that he may recognize as valid, either for others or even for himself. In so doing, he must always be ready to recognize and to accept such reasons if they are given to him.

But because of his familiarity with the subject, the humanist does not expect that he will receive reasons that he can accept, nor does he expect that he will often receive reasons that he will recognize as valid for others than himself. The humanist is expecting that the reasons given will usually be invalidated by misuses and abuses of language, which misuses and abuses the humanist must detect and demonstrate to his interlocutor. Thus the humanist must continue to discuss the abortion question by showing how the reasons given remain inadequate for himself and for others.

If the humanist's argument must consist in stating that he sees no reasons to oppose abortion, then what sort of reasons is he expecting? Those reasons must be the only kind of reasons that justify any action: it is that they serve one's interests and produce the goods to satisfy the needs as dictated by one's desires and feelings. And thus abortion may only be reasonably opposed by someone if it is contrary to his interests.

While he discusses abortion, the humanist will be confronted by many reasons which do not explicitly refer to one's interests. The humanist must explore these reasons with his interlocutor to find how they ultimately express one's interests. The humanist must point out to his interlocutor that, until such an explanation is found, his reasons cannot be considered as true reasons and that, therefore, his interlocutor is lacking a valid reason to oppose abortion.

And when the humanist has achieved this understanding with his interlocutor, the humanist has achieved the purpose of his dialogue.

Of course it is impossible, in the context of a book, to demonstrate such a dialogue. This is so because such a dialogue has never truly occurred so that it may be copied. And it is very difficult to imagine such a dialogue: very few people can pretend to play effectively both roles in the dialogue and to develop the genuine arguments of a believer when, in fact, they do not believe: the humanist should not attempt to do so, as he will surely be accused of misrepresenting his potential interlocutors.

The only demonstration of humanism in action that may be done at this time is to consider the main arguments that have been presented in the past and to comment upon them. Such a comment would give an idea of the responses that would be possible in a true dialogue.

This approach may particularly serve a useful purpose at this time: since abortion is so typical of the moral issues that are of interest to humanism, this approach will provide an opportunity to articulate an outline of humanist thought applied in a practical way. As a result, this exercise will contribute to the effectiveness of all future dialogues about many possible religious subjects. This is so because it will have responded in advance to many of the possible nonhumanist comments that could be encountered in such dialogues.

7

HUMANISM IN ACTION

There is no doubt that the main argument being offered in opposition to abortion is that there is a natural law which grants a natural right to life to every human being. This argument particularly deserves humanist consideration because it brings forth ideas which are far wider in effects than the abortion debate. The idea of natural laws and natural rights are pervasive in our society, where they represent a very decidedly anti-humanist bias, and it is these ideas that the humanist must challenge above all.

The ideas of natural laws and natural rights rest on the assumption that there are laws and rights which exist in nature independent of any human being, that these laws and rights are more or less manifest in nature, that human beings may discover and see them by studying and examining nature, and that, having done so, they are obligated to conform their behavior to these laws and to grant these rights to others while they may also claim them for themselves.

The humanist does not merely challenge the existence of natural laws and natural rights but he proposes that the very idea of such laws and rights is absurd. To do so, the humanist must explain that the ideas of natural laws and natural rights imply the ideas of absolute laws and absolute rights and he must affirm that there are no such laws and rights but that there are only relative laws and relative rights.

First, let us consider *laws.*

We have already considered *moral laws,* which we have defined as resolutions that are made by human beings to compensate for the illusion of the perspective of time, and to allow these individuals to choose the more distant satisfaction when it is judged that, in spite of appearances, it is greater than the more immediate satisfaction.

Then what are laws generally? The humanist proposes that the most simple definition of a law is that it is a statement which predicts an event. The humanist proposes that this definition is applicable to all laws. It is applicable to moral laws as well as to laws about Nature. Thus a moral law predicts that one will find a choice preferable to another choice in spite of appearances. Laws about Nature predict that under given circumstances an event will occur in Nature.

It is noteworthy that we have mentioned *laws about Nature.* This was done because laws are *about Nature* and never of Nature. It is laws *of Nature* that are implied by the idea of natural laws.

It is because laws are statements and predictions that the idea of natural laws, understood as laws *of Nature,* is absurd. It is only conscious beings who may make statements and predictions. And, because Nature is not a conscious being, it cannot make statements and predictions. Conscious beings may make statements and predictions about Nature, but these statements and predictions do not exist before someone makes them and they do not exist in Nature after they are made, except as the expressions of conscious beings. Thus laws are of conscious beings but never of Nature. Thus the idea of natural laws can only be meaningful when it is understood as laws of conscious beings about Nature.

If laws do not exist in Nature but only as expressions of the minds of conscious beings, then human beings cannot look at Nature to discover laws; but they may only observe events in Nature and then, as a result of a rational process establishing a relationship of causes and effects between these events, they may try to predict other events. And, when human beings predict these events, they are *creating* laws about Nature. And the validity of the laws is in the accuracy of the predictions. Thus, every law is a prediction and is potentially invalid.

But, if moral laws and laws about Nature are predictions, then what about political laws? It is easy to object that political laws are commands rather than predictions. But nothing prevents a law from being at once a command and a prediction. And this is particularly the nature of political laws, so that political laws like all laws are indeed predictions.

A political law always predicts that one of two things will occur. A political law is first an affirmation, by someone, that he desires that someone else act or not act in a given way and a prediction that he will act or not act in the desired way. Thus a political law always implies at least two individuals, one acting as the lawmaker whose desires must be satisfied and the other acting as the subject of the law who must satisfy the desires of the lawmaker.

But, then, the subject may not himself desire to satisfy the desires of the lawmaker. And more often than not this will be the case, so that more often than not the prediction will not come true and the law will be invalid. This is why the political law must always comprise an alternative prediction about the action of the lawmaker in the event that the subject does *not* act or does *not* not act, as desired. And, by this prediction, the lawmaker will state that he will be capable of administering a punishment to the subject who will not conform to the law and that he will be willing to administer this punishment if necessary. Of course the alternative prediction may be merely implied, but it is there nonetheless.

Thus a political law is different from other laws in that its prediction is necessarily an alternative, but then it is like any other law in that it can only be valid if its prediction comes true. Thus a political law may only be valid to the extent that the subject behaves as desired or that the lawmaker is capable of inflicting and willing to inflict the punishment that he has threatened to inflict.

Once we have mentioned the idea of political laws, we may easily move to the idea of rights. This is so because political laws imply the ideas of rights and duties. A political law is at once a statement of the duties of the subject and of the rights of the lawmaker. It is at once such a statement because the duties of one constitute the rights of the other.

Thus political laws create rights and duties. And it is obvious that duties cannot exist without political laws. One would not have a duty if it were not imposed by someone else through a political law. It is true that people speak of self-imposed duties: but such "duties" are primarily the expression of one's desires and feelings, rather than the expression of others' desires and feelings, and as such they are not truly duties.

But, if duties cannot truly exist without a political law, the same is not true of rights. Rights may exist without a political law because a right is first an affirmation about oneself. Thus, if one may affirm something about oneself, in relation to someone else, as is done in a political law, it is also possible to affirm something about oneself without implying someone else, but by implying the absence of someone else and, thus, by denying the possibility of a political law.

Then what is a right? A right may be defined as a statement expressing what one may do or not do, as well as what one may have done or not have done by others.

But one cannot express what one may do or not do, or have done or not have done, if one may not do or may not not do, or not have done or not not have done. That would simply be to express an untruth.

But why would one be able to do or not do, have done or not have done? This question cannot be answered without stating the obvious tautology that one may do or not do, have done or not have done, because one has the power to do or not do, have done or not have done.

But this tautology is not meaningless, as tautologies should be, because it must be used in the only way that a tautology may be used: it must be used to contradict one of the most common anti-humanist self-contradictions prevailing in our society, which is that "right is not might." When one states that one has the power to do something, one states that one has the might to do something. And when one recognizes that to have the right is to have the power, one recognizes that to have a right is to have might and that "right is might" and that "might is right."

And it is for this reason that the idea of natural right is absurd, if by natural right we mean that one has a right which is independent of any might. The idea that human beings have inalienable rights is absurd because experience contradicts this statement: all rights are alienable and have been alienated at one time or another!

Then, when one claims a right, one is necessarily claiming might. And, when one denies another a right, one is necessarily claiming that one has a might and that another has not.

But one will not claim a right for oneself and deny a right and impose a duty upon another merely because one has the might and another is so deprived but because one has a reason for doing so. But why would one claim a right for oneself and deny it to another if not for the same reason that one performs any action, which is to serve one's interests and to produce the good to satisfy one's needs as dictated by one's desires and feelings?

But, as we have seen, an individual sometimes serves his own interests indirectly by serving the interests of another. Because of this, rights are not only claimed for oneself but may also be granted to another, in which case one assumes as a self-imposed "duty" to serve another. And, when this occurs, another may claim the rights that are granted to him through one's might: in this case, one's might becomes his might.

Thus it is possible for rights to be granted. But not all rights are granted. Yet, this is an implied belief of our society which is often expressed by the question: "What gives you the right to do so-and-so?" As rights are firstly affirmations about oneself, and as rights exist by default of a greater might, then the individual alone has all the rights to do and not do everything that is within his own personal capacity to do or not do. Thus it is only because of others that the rights of that individual, to do what he may otherwise do or not do, may be limited.

And just as rights exist by default of a greater might that would limit them, so duties can only exist, in spite of the individual's feelings and desires, if there is a greater might that would impose them, and the individual alone cannot have duties which are in conflict with his feelings and desires.

Once it is understood that there are no natural laws that grant natural rights but that all rights are expressions of might, it is possible to consider the question of abortion in a new light.

The first fact that must be recognized is that the unborn, who exists as a powerless appendage of someone else, is incapable of conceiving of rights and of life, much less of choosing to live or not to live. For this reason, the concept of rights does not apply to him, and it is as meaningless to say that he does not have a right as it is to say that he has such a right.

The second fact that must be recognized is that the mother has an interest to either continue or terminate her pregnancy, depending on her feelings and desires. But does she have the right? She does by default, unless it is denied to her by someone who has an interest in doing so as well as a greater power than the mother's. And this individual may not only compel the mother to continue her pregnancy to term, contrary to her desire, but he may compel her to terminate it when she wishes to continue it!

But who has such an interest? The father will often feel that he has such an interest, sometimes to see the mother undergo an abortion and, at other times, to see her carry the child to term. But does he have the right? Which is to say: Is the father capable of compelling the mother to do as he wishes? This question cannot be answered except in relation to each actual case. Obviously, society will be a factor in determining the rights of the father and of the mother. But why would society intervene? And why would society choose to grant the right to the father rather than to the mother and to impose a burden upon the mother to serve the interests of the father? What difference does it make to society that "he is the father"?

These are the questions that the humanist and those who are not opposed to abortion should be asking of those who support laws that would forbid abortion. The latter would have more difficulties in answering the questions if they can no longer claim that they are acting without personal interests and that they are merely supporting a natural right which is granted by virtue of a natural law.

It is indicative of the intellectual weakness of those who do not oppose abortion that they have not challenged their opponents' belief in natural laws and natural rights but that they have rather reinforced such a belief. This is what they have done when they have claimed, in spite of the existence of political laws that forbid abortion, that "women have a right to abortion." They cannot ignore the existence of political laws and proclaim such a right without implying that such a right is a "natural right" which can only ensue from a "natural law" which would be "superior" to any possible political law and which would invalidate it. They cannot do so without agreeing with their opponents exactly when they should not!

* * *

Those who oppose abortion and claim a right to life for the unborn are not claiming such a right for all beings but only for human beings. In fact, many of them will accept and even defend the right of human beings to kill the nonhuman. Some will be more squeamish about it and will demand that a human being show a purpose for so doing, but they will recognize many purposes as valid, such as the need to feed and to clothe oneself.

The fact that they make a distinction between human and nonhuman lives implies that human life has a special value which grants it an inherent sacredness. It is for this reason that they feel that they need only state that the unborn is a human being to have stated their case and to have proved that the unborn should not be aborted. They feel that merely to have shown photographs of aborted fetuses, to demonstrate the appearance of a human form, is enough to have proved their point.

And, having demonstrated that the unborn is human, those who oppose abortion have felt free to claim that abortion is infanticide and murder and to brand those who perform abortions, as well as those who undergo abortions, as child killers and murderers who must be prevented from performing their wretched deeds by every means or who must be punished for having done so.

Those who would allow abortions have truly been intimidated by these arguments. They have so lacked in intellectual wakefulness that they have accepted as self-evident that human life is inherently sacred, and thus they have been condemned to defend their point and to deny that abortion is murder and infanticide by denying the self-evident, which is that the unborn is human. They have been reduced to being apologetic about their stand and to diverting attention from the subject of abortion: this is what they are doing when they speak of unwanted children and of birth control.

The humanist can only view this disarray with sorrow, and it is to straighten it out that his intervention is so sorely needed. And, by this intervention, the humanist will consider the arguments of those who oppose abortion and he will show how they are speaking meaninglessly and how they are failing to say why they oppose abortion.

The humanist will not challenge the belief that the unborn is a human being. To the contrary, the humanist will agree with those who oppose abortion that the unborn is a human being from conception, and even before conception. The humanist will recognize that this is true tautologically, and that an unborn human being is a human being (and, more precisely, that it is an *unborn human being*!) and that those who are in favor of allowing abortion are self-contradictory in denying it.

What the humanist challenges is the belief that the unborn should not be aborted because he is human and the belief that it is self-evident that human life has a special value which grants it an inherent sacredness. Such a belief implies a serious misunderstanding of the meaning of value. This belief, in claiming a self-evident value, is implying an absolute and objective value, and the humanist will deny that the value of human life is absolute and objective.

Value means *worth* and, as such, always implies an equation of something measured in terms of something else and in relation to someone in particular. Thus there is no absolute value, and it is meaningless to speak of the value of human life without stating the terms of that value, and for whom it is so valuable. For this reason, it is meaningless to speak of human life in the abstract, and it is only possible to speak of the value of each individual's life to himself and to others. And this value varies with each life and with each person, as he has appraised it subjectively in terms of his feelings and desires. And it may be worthless or less than worthless to the individual who finds that suicide is the best option for him. Thus the value of one's life does not come from the fact that one is human, but from the fact that one is oneself and that one desires to live, and, if one were a cow, and one would want to live, then one would still value one's life.

Thus the humanist must deny the meaningfulness of absolute and objective value and, when confronted by the idea of the value of human life, he must ask, "What is the value of what life, for whom, and to what purpose?"

As value must be appraised and requires a conscious effort, it is meaningless to speak of the value of human life to the unborn, who is incapable of making such an appraisal. The value of the unborn can only be his value to someone other than himself. One of these individuals other than himself will certainly be his mother and, depending on the circumstances, the value of her unborn child may be negative. Then why should she not be allowed to have an abortion?

The humanist will not deny that abortion is infanticide. The humanist may propose that, inasmuch as "an infant" is by definition "a born child," then abortion cannot be infanticide. But the humanist will not belabor this explanation. If others want to claim that an unborn child is an infant, then the humanist can accept this definition because it is unimportant. It is so because it is meaningless for humanist purpose. Thus to say that abortion is infanticide because the unborn is an infant is to state a tautology which is to say nothing.

It is also meaningless to state that abortion is murder. Murder is often understood to be the killing of a human being. If that is so, then to say that abortion is murder, like saying that it is infanticide, is tautological and meaningless.

But people who oppose abortion often recognize that there are instances when they do not oppose the killing of a human being and when they refuse to accept that such killings are murders. To satisfy these people, then murder must be defined differently. And the humanist must agree that a definition, implying that murder is a special kind of killing, is more in keeping with the usual meaning of the word. And what may be the characteristic of that kind of killing that differentiates it from other kinds of killings? The humanist proposes that it is that "one is opposed to it." Thus murder is a killing particularly defined from a subjective and negative point of view. It is "a killing to which one is opposed." But then to say that one is opposed to abortion because it is murder is to say that one is opposed to abortion because it is a killing to which one is opposed, which again is to say exactly nothing.

Thus the humanist has not denied that the unborn is a human being, nor that abortion is infanticide or murder: what the humanist has done by explaining these words is to show that those who oppose abortion, in claiming that the unborn is a human being and that his killing is infanticide and murder, have been speaking meaninglessly and have in fact failed to state why they oppose abortion!

*   *   *

Ultimately, there is only one reason that one should do anything, and that is that it serves one's interests by producing the good to satisfy one's needs as dictated by one's feelings and desires. Such is the essence of humanist morality.

Among those who oppose abortion there are some who do so on the basis of the humanist principle and while claiming that abortion is contrary to one's interests. Again, there are those who oppose abortion for non-humanist reasons, which is without reference to one's interests. Finally, there are others who take a stand which is definitely anti-humanist and who imply that one should not serve one's interests.

This is what the latter are doing, consciously or not, when they accuse women who are seeking abortions of doing so for selfish and frivolous reasons and of submitting to abortions for reasons of convenience.

The humanist will not argue whether abortion or any action is frivolous: whatever is frivolous is a matter of personal and subjective taste and no one may agree about it, but it is up to each individual to decide for himself. However, the humanist must certainly comment about the selfishness of abortion and affirm that there is no more justifiable reason to seek abortion, or anything else, than one's convenience. If an action does not ultimately lead to one's good, such an action has no reason to be performed. That abortion leads to that good immediately is the clearest indication that it is reasonable and eminently moral.

Having said so, the humanist cannot say much more to those who oppose abortion for anti-humanist reasons. And he may now undertake to consider the arguments of those who oppose abortion for nonhumanist reasons, which are reasons unrelated to one's interests. This is the case with the arguments that the medical practitioners are forbidden by the terms of their professional oath to perform abortions and that the medical profession and facilities should not perform or be used to perform abortions because "pregnancy is neither a disease nor an injury."

With respect to the Hippocratic oath, the humanist will point out that this oath acts as a moral law and that, as such, it is subject to evaluation as to its purpose and to change so as to better serve that purpose. Thus the humanist will then question whether this oath, in forbidding abortion, serves the purpose that a moral law should serve, which is to guide individuals to the greatest satisfaction of their needs, and therefore whether it deserves to continue to be respected or whether it should be reworded to better fit its purpose or, yet, whether it should not be completely ignored.

With respect to the use of the medical profession and facilities, the humanist will point out that, when it is proposed that the medical profession and facilities should not be used to terminate pregnancies because the latter are not diseases or injuries, it is assumed that the medical profession and facilities are, by definition, designed to cure diseases and to treat injuries. And it is quite possible that one would be inclined to give such a definition if one did not think too much about it.

But, on second thought, one must recognize that a profession and facilities are not designed to serve definitions but to serve people and, if their usual definitions prove inadequate to describe the services that they may render to people, then one should not restrict their functions to fit the definitions but one should rather change their definitions to allow them to perform the full functions that they are capable of performing. As the practice of abortion, as well as that of plastic surgery, becomes more and more prevalent in our society, it is obvious that the functions of the medical profession and facilities will change and that their definitions must necessarily reflect this fact.

Thus, the Hippocratic oath and the definitions of the medical profession and facilities are merely words which must serve as means and which can only be valid as long as they serve the desired ends. If these words should serve to forbid abortion contrary to one's desire, then one has ceased to use words to serve one's purpose but has allowed oneself to become the victim of the words that one uses.

Having disposed of the anti-humanist and nonhumanist arguments, the humanist must now consider the arguments of those who claim that they are serving their interests by opposing abortion. The humanist must accept that such interests might exist and he must consider carefully the reasons that are given to him.

But, before he does so, the humanist must point out that these reasons are more or less subjective and objective, and he must show the implications of this fact.

A reason is objective to the extent that it is shared by others, while it is subjective to the extent that it is not. A reason will be shared with more difficulty as it is more closely related to one's desires and feelings, as it is related to an end and to an ultimate end rather than to a means, as it is a reason which is without a further reason.

A reason will be more or less shared depending on the individuals involved. Thus it is possible for individuals to share the same feeling. However, if they do not, there is very little that can be done that will lead them to share it.

It is a lot easier for individuals to share a reason which is not directly related to feelings. This is possible because people will share such a reason merely by recognizing a relationship of causes and effects. Thus it is often possible for a person to convince another to accept such a reason merely by talking to him and showing him a possible relationship of which he is not aware.

Let us first consider the subjective reasons. Obviously, the most subjective reason to oppose abortion would be an overwhelming feeling of compassion for the unborn. The feeling may be so strong that one feels compelled to prevent others by every means from submitting to abortion, or from performing abortions. The humanist must recognize that this feeling is genuine and that those who oppose abortion are truly serving their interests in doing so. But, while he recognizes this fact, the humanist must stress the subjectivity and privacy of the feeling and must not allow those who oppose abortion to claim that their feeling is objective and public and that it should therefore be shared by anyone else and, much less, by everyone else.

In fact, the humanist must point out that the feeling against abortion is not essentially different from any other feeling. Although these feelings may be different from one another and even opposite to one another, they are all alike in their genesis: they all have their source in the origins and past of the individuals. And each of these feelings is at once subjectively good and bad for different individuals at the same time. Thus, while one may abhor abortion, one cannot expect that another will not enjoy performing or undergoing an abortion and one has no justification to claim that his own feelings are objectively better than another's.

But the fact that the reason is subjective does not mean that one will be inhibited from imposing it upon others through political laws. We must remember that all political laws, like all human actions, must rest ultimately on one's feelings and desires.

But, in spite of that, most human beings like to believe that they share a reason for their actions and that they do not need to compel others to act as they would have them do but that they can convince them to do so. This is why those who oppose abortion like to claim that their opposition to abortion is merely a means to an end and that the end is one which is so broad in scope that it is shared by most everyone.

And among the objective reasons to oppose abortion is the claim that a law against abortion is in effect a moral law which demands an immediate sacrifice in exchange for a later and greater good, and they will propose that a collective law against abortion would ultimately protect everyone's life.

If this were true, then most everyone would have a clear, explicit, and objective reason to oppose abortion and to support such a law. But how true is it? Is it true that the rights of all are threatened when the rights of one are threatened and, thus, that abortion threatens all human beings, that it will lead inexorably to euthanasia and to compulsory euthanasia?

The humanist must contest this argument in two ways. First, he must point out that the rights of everyone are always threatened and that they are not threatened because the rights of another are threatened but because might is right and because one is never sure that might is not against one.

Thus it is not because of abortion that one's right to life is threatened but it is in the nature of rights and of life to be always threatened.

The humanist must also respond to this argument by challenging the assumption that human beings are condemned to make absolute laws that forbid them to do what they want to do, so that they will not do what they do not want to do, and that they cannot improve their laws by stating exceptions within the terms of the laws.

Thus, while it is true that human beings will make and support collective laws that will protect them from each other, and that they will support these laws, even though these laws are not in their interests in the short run, because they can see a greater benefit in the long run, there is a point where such laws cease to be beneficial and begin to be a burden. And reasonable people will try to improve such laws by stating the exceptions that will retain the benefits while removing the ill effects. And such a law is certainly the law that forbids killing of human beings, when considered with respect to the unborn. It is self-evident that people do not need to make a law that would forbid killing and that would protect the unborn, because such a law would not further protect those who are born since they will never again be unborn.

Furthermore, the law allowing abortion cannot in any way lead to a law allowing the killing of the old and the sick. This is true because, while the lawmaker is sure that he will never be unborn again, he also knows that he will probably be old or sick someday and that such a law would threaten him.

Again, the argument that we will never again be unborn may be invoked against those who are scandalized that unborn are killed by abortion while murderers are spared capital punishment. Again, while everyone knows that he will never be unborn, he is not sure that, one day, in a moment of uncontrollable anger, he will not kill, or that, even worse, he will not be falsely accused and found guilty of such an act, and thus capital punishment threatens all born human beings while abortion does not. This reasoning does not mean that one should be opposed to capital punishment, but only that one has fewer rather than more reasons to oppose abortion than to oppose capital punishment.

We have argued that abortion does not lead us necessarily against our will to euthanasia, but in so doing we do not admit directly or indirectly that we should not want euthanasia. Just as suicide may be the best alternative when one's life has become a net liability, so euthanasia may be the most desirable alternative that society must take in particular for deficient newborns and for those who no longer function as conscious beings. But this is another question.

Having disposed of the major reasons of those who oppose abortion, the humanist must finally consider the reason that many of these people refuse to use and which is probably their most objective reason to oppose abortion. This reason is a belief in a God that commands one to oppose abortion and that can enforce His command and severely punish the law-breakers. And to those atheists who would allow abortion, we must add that the belief in such a divine law is far more reasonable than the belief in a natural law: inasmuch as such a God is conceived as a person, then divine law is not implicitly an absurdity.

But, then, admitting that such a God exists, why would He make a law forbidding abortion? What are His reasons and what interests is He serving? However, the humanist might never discuss these questions with the people who oppose abortion. This is so because the humanist would certainly want, first, to question the existence of such a God and, second, to question that He has made such a law. And, if the humanist should ever agree that there is such a God and that He has made such a law, it is with God rather than with anyone else that he would want to discuss the reasons for such a law!

PART FOUR

THE HUMANIST CITY

8

THE HUMANIST SOCIETY

The history of human society is the history of persecution and torture, war and destruction, maiming and killing, treachery, plunder and slavery, among other misfortunes. And, while every individual abhors this fate and hopes that it will not be his, many have been its victims, and everyone is always threatened of becoming so.

How has this been possible? How can human beings be led to suffer a fate that they abhor? Humanism proposes that this has been made possible by the nature of human society and that this possibility can be further reinforced by anti-humanism, which can make it its mission to promote such a fate.

The overriding fact that affects the nature of human society is that such a society is composed of different individuals who seek to serve their different interests. And it is these different interests which are often in conflict, wherein lies the seed of all the ills of human society.

Human society is like every other animal society. In fact, it is a component of the larger animal society where everyone seeks to eat and not be eaten. And human society is even more treacherous than the larger animal society. This is so because the human needs are much more numerous and varied and thus the possibility of conflicts is also much greater than for other animals.

And this is why, by its nature, human society constitutes a war of all against all. But, then, how can it survive its nature? How is human society at all possible?

It can only be possible if there is a mechanism at work within it that can serve to reduce the number and intensity of the conflicts within it. And this mechanism exists: it is *leadership*.

Without leadership, human society would not be possible. Thus leadership is not something that a human society may acquire or dispense itself with. Leadership is an unavoidable and necessary condition of every human society, however small or large it may be.

Even if it were possible to imagine a human society without leadership, such a society could not remain in this condition for very long. In such a society, there would be no peace and security, and even the strongest individuals would never know when they would be struck down by treacherous blows. In such a society, everyone would want to destroy others before he is destroyed by them. Such a society would destroy itself, or else leadership would emerge within it from one or more of the wilier individuals and it would be gladly accepted by almost everyone in the hope that it would implant peace and security.

Leadership is essential to any society because of the need to reduce the number of conflicts of interest within it and leadership serves this function by endeavoring to provide solutions to such conflicts.

Leaders resolve conflicts of interest by establishing the rights of everyone. But, to do so, they must first set aside one right for their own exclusive exercise. And this right, which leaders monopolize and which serve to implant peace and security within society, is the exclusive right to use violence and to permit and order the use of violence. Thus the leaders mobilize the strength of everyone against anyone that offends the established rights and against anyone who uses violence without permission.

But leaders cannot always monopolize violence and guarantee peace and security. This is due to the fact that the leaders have their own interests and will use their prerogative to compel their subjects to serve these interests.

This, in itself, will not threaten peace and security, because the people will be ready to tolerate some measure of exploitation from their leaders in exchange for the peace and security that it otherwise provides. But the leaders will often be greedy and impose suffering beyond what many individuals will tolerate: it is this condition that will then prove to be an opportunity for enterprising individuals to rise and challenge the leaders.

These challengers will gather the support of the most dissatisfied individuals and, together, the challengers and their supporters will be able to terrorize a large number of otherwise indifferent individuals into collaborating with them to harass the leaders.

Leaders who are threatened by such challenges will become suspicious of everyone and they will direct repressive action against anyone whom they suspect of supporting their challengers. Every criticism of the leaders will then become suspicious. But then even the appearance of criticizing the leaders will also be considered as suspicious. Thus any expression of dissatisfaction with one's fate may be construed as an expression that the leaders have failed at their task and that, therefore, they should be overthrown. Thus, eventually, the subjects will be reluctant to express their feelings and desires for fear that it will be interpreted as an expression of dissatisfaction and as a justification of, and support for, the challengers.

This is how the struggle for leadership within society often leads to a civil war, and the people, who are merely the unwilling and helpless pawns and victims of the protagonists, must bear all the suffering that such a condition entails.

This condition will last until the challengers and their supporters are defeated, or until the leaders are overthrown, when the challengers become the new leaders, and this condition will repeat itself as soon as new challengers arise to confront the winners.

And the leaders, when they exploit and repress the people, and the challengers, when they terrorize the people into collaborating with them, are often reinforced by anti-humanist religions that can impose moralities of meaninglessness and self-contradictions that can support these individuals and their actions.

But what will the anti-humanist religions do to justify the leaders, or the challengers, as they impose suffering upon the people? Obviously, they will abuse the most important word in relation to morality and they will propose that "suffering is good." They will make goodness into an absolute and objective thing independent of the individual, so that individuals may be asked to seek goodness while not seeking their own good.

Such religions will claim that the purpose of each individual human being is to serve something "bigger than himself," such as a God, or an ideology, or a political party, or a social class, or a state, or a country, or even of the whole of humanity, and that it is one or more of these things which are absolutely good and that the individual can only be good himself in a relative way in serving them and that he must gladly accept and bear the sacrifices and suffering that ensue from this service.

Such religions will then justify the leaders, or the challengers, when they sacrifice the people to their interests by explaining that the leaders, or the challengers, are the agents of Absolute Goodness and that the interests of the leaders, or the challengers, are the interests of Goodness and that anyone who opposes the leaders, or the challengers, is in fact opposing Goodness and is therefore acting immorally and deserves to be punished.

Such religions will also reinforce their own point by claiming that conflict is in the nature of society and therefore that it is unavoidable and by claiming that all conflicts are ultimately part of the Great Conflict between Good and Evil and that the individual has no choice but to join one side or the other, the righteous or the wicked side, to strike and be struck and to suffer the consequences of the Conflict.

Thus individuals who have looked upon leadership to provide peace and security within society are often threatened in their peace and security by, and because of, the very leaders that they are supporting, and they are now commanded to believe that this condition must be accepted as natural and unavoidable, that they must not seek to serve their interests but that they must serve some Superior Cause and that they must do so by being unquestionably loyal and obedient to their leaders, or to the challengers.

And this is the condition which prevails unchallenged over most of the earth today, and which prevails, at least in some mitigated manner, everywhere in the world.

But how could the anti-humanist religions impose this condition upon the people?

The truth is that human beings were not exactly compelled against their will to believe that they should not seek to serve their interests but that they should rather sacrifice their interests to a "higher cause." They must certainly have slipped into anti-humanist beliefs because of their lack of intellectual awareness of what was happening. Thus, there is no doubt that, at one time, the cause that the people were serving was truly a means to serve their interests and that it is only little by little that this cause lost its purpose. But the people failed to understand that truth and to recognize the self-contradictions and meaninglessness that were creeping into their beliefs. They were rather encouraged by their political and religious leaders to maintain the True Faith. In fact, they were told, on the one hand, that they should serve the Cause because, in doing so, they were serving their interests and, on the other hand, that they should serve this Cause even when this is contrary to their interests because they should not seek to serve their interests.

Thus, for having learned to accept this self-contradiction, the people were easily convinced to identify their welfare with the Cause, sometimes in spite of all the evidence to the contrary. As a result of this conviction, they would defend their religious beliefs, as well as their religious and political leaders, against all attacks, while thinking that they were defending their very persons. And they became willing to persecute those who may have helped them.

Thus, when an individual would arise who could challenge such beliefs, he was well advised to emasculate his own beliefs so that they would not be understood, or else he would be persecuted and silenced by the religious or political leaders, with the complicity of the people, before he could express himself in a manner that could be understood.

But the power of these leaders to support anti-humanism is not invincible. In fact, in many parts of the world it is no longer absolute and it is possible for the humanist minister to express himself. And he must seize this opportunity and challenge the anti-humanist beliefs.

*   *   *

But what must the humanist minister do in relation to human society? Obviously, he must reaffirm his denial of the anti-humanist belief that the individual exists for the purpose of serving something other than himself.

And, as he does so, the humanist minister particularly denies the specific anti-humanist belief that the people exist to serve the political leaders or some of their challengers.

The humanist minister must do so, while explaining that the political leaders and the challengers will have their own point of view and that they will logically consider that the people exist to serve them, but while emphasizing that the people do not need to share the point of view of these individuals, but that, in fact, the people should consider that it is they who must be served by the leaders and challengers and that they should logically endeavor to impose their beliefs upon these individuals.

The humanist minister will then point out that the leaders must serve the people in a very particular way, which is to maintain peace and security within society by resolving conflicts of interest within it and that the leaders must never do the unthinkable and jeopardize this peace and security by provoking and promoting such conflicts. The humanist minister must proclaim this truth to the people and ensure that they are forever aware of it.

Having done so, the humanist minister must then show the people how they may compel their leaders to serve them and how they may use the very conflicts between the leaders and the challengers as a means to further serve the popular interests rather than allow such conflicts to be impediments to this end.

The humanist minister may do so by pointing out that this may be achieved if the leaders can rule only with the consent of the people, so that the people may easily dismiss the leaders and replace them by their very challengers! To bring about and maintain such a political situation, the power of the leaders must be limited so that the individuals may be allowed to express their feelings and desires and to complain about their lot, so that the people and challengers may be allowed to criticize the performance of the leaders, and so that the challengers may hope to replace the leaders without violence at those regular intervals when the people are given the opportunity to confirm the leaders in their position or to dismiss them and to replace them by some of their challengers.

Because of this opportunity, the people can hope to be served rather than exploited by the leaders. And this fact will restrict the options that are open to the challengers. The latter will have more difficulty in finding the kind of hopelessness upon which to organize a revolution and they will often be reduced to using peaceful means to displace the leaders.

Having proposed the elements of the political system upon which it is possible to found a society where the people would live in peace and security while seeking the good that would satisfy their needs as dictated by their feelings and desires and which is truly a *humanist society,* the humanist minister has not proposed some Utopian dream which is yet to become reality. Rather, he has outlined the political system which prevails, more or less, in many countries of the world today. Thus the humanist society is already a fact in our world today, although it may not yet be recognized as such.

And the reason that the humanist society is not recognized for what it is, is that it is very imperfectly so and that it is very prone to fail in its humanist purpose.

Of course the humanist society will be doomed to failure if the leaders, as well as the challengers, forever prove themselves, in turn, incompetent to perform so as to serve the people by resolving the conflicts of interest within society. The best intentions in the world will be for naught if one does not know how to achieve results. And the failure of the leaders who claim to be guided by humanist beliefs can only lend support to those who would establish an anti-humanist society.

And this is why the humanist minister must not be satisfied to affirm the popular purpose of the leaders, nor to outline the political system that would support such a purpose; he must further propose the ways and means whereby the leaders may better fulfill their role in resolving conflicts of interest. In so doing, the humanist minister is also inspiring the terms of the criticisms that the challengers must direct at the leaders, when necessary, which is to show that these ways and means are not being used as well as they should be by the incumbent leaders.

Then what solutions may the humanist minister propose?

There are more than one, but there is one which he prefers above all. What is it? What is the solution of a religion that proposes that human beings have failed to act morally, and to act in accordance with their nature and to serve their interests, because they have misused and abused language, except to find that the conflict is due to this very cause? And what solution would better resolve the conflict than to find that it is merely caused by a misuse and abuse of language? And what would be this solution except to find that there is no conflict?

Thus it is incumbent upon the leaders to ensure that there is truly no conflict, and the humanist minister must himself ensure that the leaders have fully explored the possibility of this solution, before seeking any other solution.

Thus the leaders must first seek to prove that the conflict does not exist, but that what appears to be a conflict is in fact an illusion.

Since this may be achieved by showing how the conflict is based on a misuse or abuse of language, then the correction of such misuse or abuse will by itself dissipate the conflict.

And humanism proposes that a large number of conflicts are of this kind and are capable of this solution. And, when a conflict is not of this kind, it is often *partly* of this kind and is therefore capable of a partial solution as proposed.

But a partial solution is not enough. And what about the conflicts that are not capable of the proposed solution?

Thus this solution has its limitations. If the leaders are to resolve conflicts by showing that they are illusory because they are based on misuses and abuses of language, then this must be the fact and conflicts must truly be based on such misuses and abuses. And the leader must never forget that this may not be the case!

Thus the humanist minister must not pretend that all conflicts are illusory, nor must he encourage the leaders to perform as if this were the case. The humanist minister, if he were to do so, could do no greater disservice to mankind. Nothing could be worse for a human being than to live in the self-contradictory situation of a conflict which he refuses to recognize. Such a person would soon be the victim of despair and insanity.

Thus the humanist minister must encourage the leaders to seek out true conflicts of interests where they exist, to recognize them for what they are, and to point them out as clearly as possible. And it is only for having done so that it becomes possible to resolve these conflicts satisfactorily.

But then how should leaders resolve true conflicts of interest? To do so, there are some methods which are better than others. But the best methods cannot always be used. And this is why the leaders must, in the first place, endeavor to apply the best method and must then use a less preferred method when a better one proves unworkable.

And what is the best method that may be used to eliminate a true conflict? Would it not be to prove that the conflict does not need to be resolved: to prove that the parties may agree that they do not need to agree?

And how is this possible? This is possible when it is recognized that the circumstances allow each individual to act independently of every other individual and without having to submit to the inconvenience of consulting and agreeing with anyone else.

This solution is quite often the case. It is the case whenever the good which is the cause of the conflict may be divided between the parties engaged in the conflict, so that each may do with his share as he wishes.

But, even though a large number of conflicts which are not illusory are capable of this solution, again there is a limit to the application of the formula, which again may be applicable in part or not at all. For one thing, the parties will not always agree as to how to divide the good so that each may use his share as he wishes. For another thing, many goods by their very nature cannot be divided and one or both parties can never be fully satisfied by any solution about their use.

Obviously, in these cases, each party will be inclined to use violence in order to impose his preferred solution upon his opponent. Against this inclination, the leaders must point out that the use of violence will always be detrimental to one of the parties and it will often be detrimental to both, so that each party will usually come out the poorer because of it. This is why the leaders must affirm their resolve to prevent violence and to seek a peaceful resolution of the conflict. Such a resolution can only be achieved by means of negotiations whereby each party must surrender some of his claim regarding the division or use of the good.

Thus, when the leaders have recognized that the conflict is neither illusory nor unnecessary, they must enjoin the parties to negotiate. But then they must do more. They must observe the negotiations and ensure that they are fruitful. And, whenever they see that the progress of the negotiations is in difficulty, they must endeavor to show to the parties, with concrete propositions, how successful negotiations may be achieved, and they must offer to act as mediators in the conflict.

The leaders, in promoting negotiations, are aware that talk will not necessarily guarantee understanding, but they also are aware that failure to talk will guarantee misunderstanding.

Thus, in spite of the best efforts of the leaders, it will happen that the parties will refuse to agree to mutual concessions and, thus, a solution by negotiation will prove to be impossible. In such a situation, the leaders must recognize that the second method is also unworkable and they must resort to the third and least desirable kind of solution, which is to dictate the terms of the solution to the parties.

In favoring one or the other party, the leaders must consider the possibility that one of them might have refused the application of a better solution. Thus it is possible that one of the parties, because of intellectual limitations, refuses to recognize that the conflict is illusory or unnecessary or negotiable, while the leaders, and possibly the other party, do. In such a situation, the leaders should attempt to impose the better solution.

However, to do so may not always be the wiser alternative. This is so when the party that would be favored by such a solution does not have a great desire for the good in question, while the other party does. In such a situation, the satisfaction of the latter party would normally constitute a greater contribution to peace and security and the wise leaders should recognize this and should act in consequence. But, having done so, the leaders must endeavor to overcome the intellectual limitations of this party so that it may be possible, in the future, to apply a better solution.

Thus, in favoring one or the other party, the leaders must always recognize that individuals may not have equal desires of the good and they must endeavor to obtain a balance of satisfaction while providing the greatest possible satisfaction for each individual. Thus they must endeavor to recognize and satisfy the greatest desires in each circumstance, bearing in mind that the accumulation of numerous smaller dissatisfactions will add up to a large dissatisfaction.

Of course the problem of evaluating the desires of others is no simple matter, since each desire is largely subjective and the individual who desires is by far the most competent to perform this evaluation. But it is of little use for the leaders to ask the conflicting parties to express the magnitude of their desires, since each party would have an interest to lie and to claim that his own desires are the greatest. Thus the leaders must guess the relative values of the desires of each individual, based on circumstantial evidences, and must adjudicate as best he can. This evaluation will seldom be perfect, so that some individuals will often feel cheated by it.

In order to alleviate the ill feelings of the party that feels cheated by the judgment, the leaders must stand ready to try to explain that judgment to this party. But the fact that they must explain their judgment does not mean that action upon it must await a satisfactory explanation, else it would never be carried out. Thus, while they explain their judgment, the leaders must be ready to enforce it. Thus, should one of the parties choose to resort to violence because of his dissatisfaction, the leaders must be ready to confront this violence with the necessary force to dissuade this party of his intentions.

The leaders, inspired by humanist beliefs, must be unhappy when they use force, because they know that such actions, if repeated, will soon destroy the peace and security that they want to maintain in society. But, while they are unhappy about their action, they must not hesitate to perform it, because they know that failure to do so will also destroy this peace and security and that it will do so immediately!

Thus it is not the willingness to use force, to impose a solution to a conflict, that characterizes anti-humanist leadership, but it is this willingness to do so without having exhausted the alternatives and having sought to prove, in turn, that the conflict was either illusory or unnecessary or negotiable. Once the leaders have truly tried and failed to provide such a proof, and once they have recognized that the conflict can only be resolved by adjudication, their unwillingness to provide this adjudication and to enforce it would not raise a question about their status as humanists but rather about their status as leaders. And no leader, including those who claim to be guided by humanist beliefs, can afford to allow this to happen.

* * *

But conflicts within society do not only occur between individuals, but often they occur between groups of individuals.

The idea of groups adds its own complexity to the problems of leadership. Superficially, the solution to these problems seems easy. Thus, if the leaders are to provide the greatest possible satisfaction, is it not logical that they should satisfy the larger groups to the detriment of the lesser groups?

Humanism proposes that this solution, which is often considered to be the *democratic solution,* implies a misunderstanding of the meaning of *democracy* and constitutes, to an extent, a failure of democracy and of humanistic leadership.

Then what is the meaning of democracy?

Democracy has been identified at once as *liberty* and as *majority rule.* But liberty and majority rule are not synonymous: they may in fact be antonymous! Thus, by its very nature, to rule is to limit the freedom of those that are ruled and majority rule limits the freedom of the minority.

Thus, when people speak of democracy, meaning at once liberty and majority rule, they are speaking in self-contradictory terms.

Then what does democracy mean? Is it liberty or is it majority rule? Or is it something different yet?

Humanism proposes that democracy is, by definition, "the government of the people by the people," which means "the government of *all* the people by *all* the people," that it is only by virtue of an evolution of meaning that democracy has come to mean "the government of *all* the people by the *majority* of the people," and that it is only by returning to its original definition that it is possible to identify democracy with freedom.

Obviously, a "government of all the people by all the people" is practically impossible since it requires a unanimity of purpose that can be found in few societies. Thus democracy is an ideal to be sought after and to be achieved as much as possible without expectation of perfection.

And it is this ideal that is the goal of humanism when it proposes that the humanist society is one which is democratic or which, at least, endeavors to be democratic. And such a society will endeavor to be democratic if its government endeavors to satisfy all groups and all individuals within these groups rather than one or some at the expense of the others.

But, if humanism must deal effectively with groups within society, it must recognize that the presence of large groups within society constitutes by itself a threat to peace and security. This is so because such groups can provide the ready-made support that challengers need to confront the leaders, and challengers will often seek the leadership of some of these groups to improve their strength. The leaders will then be compelled to assume the leadership of the opposing groups to better confront these challengers. And this polarization within society can only lead to a civil war, hence the threat to peace and security.

Thus, if peace and security must be maintained within society, then the danger of the polarization of society must be recognized and met. And this is a role that the humanist minister is particularly capable of performing.

To do so, the humanist minister must first minimize the importance of the groups. The humanist minister must do so by stressing the importance of the individual and the fact that there is no meaningful satisfaction unless it is ultimately the satisfaction of the individuals. The humanist minister must point out the obvious corollary to the humanist beliefs about human nature and purpose, which is that groups, like everything else, can only exist ultimately to serve the individuals and that the individuals can never be expected to consider themselves to exist to serve the groups, as has often been the case in human history.

The humanist minister must then suggest that the interests of the individuals as members of groups are often greatly exaggerated to the detriment of the true interests of the individuals independent of the groups.

The humanist minister must then explain that the importance of the groups is diminished by the fact that individuals have numerous needs, each in relation to a separate good, and that each good will generate its own set of opposing groups. Thus individuals may belong to a number of groups, so that few individuals can share all the same common interests and so that they cannot coalesce on one point without being in conflict on another, and this fact will militate against the possibility of a strong polarization within society and thus should be welcome and promoted by the humanist minister and the leaders who would be guided by humanist beliefs.

Thus the humanist minister should attempt to depolarize the people, until the distinction between groups is blurred as much as possible, by making it so that the alignment of individuals is different for each different conflict and so that no group of individuals can find that it has so many common interests that it must coalesce against everyone else.

To further help along the depolarization of society, the humanist minister must discourage the use of labels of polarization, such as *rightist* and *leftist, radical* and *reactionary, conservative* and *liberal.* The humanist minister must even discourage the use of *humanism* and *anti-humanism* as such labels and must suggest that individuals should speak in terms of their individual needs rather than in terms of religious and political ideologies which often lead individuals to commit themselves to groups that then become ends in themselves, independent of the individuals, and that work against the best interests of the individuals while demanding and enforcing the latter's unfailing allegiance.

Such is the approach of humanism with respect to groups.

But what is the anti-humanist approach? What should we expect from the anti-humanist?

Of course the anti-humanist, in proposing that individuals should not seek to serve their interests but that they should endeavor to serve the interests of some Absolute Goodness, must postulate that every conflict of interest is not primarily between individuals but rather between Absolute Goodness and Absolute Wickedness. Having done so, anti-humanism cannot accept that different individuals will be opposed on different issues, but must demand that all individuals who stand for Absolute Goodness must agree on all questions, as dictated by Absolute Goodness, and must be opposed on every question to all those who stand for Absolute Wickedness. Thus the anti-humanist society must be polarized into two conflicting and irreconcilable groups, one the righteous, the other the wicked, both opposed to each other on every issue and condemned to struggle against each other until the other, the wicked one, is overcome and destroyed.

Obviously, in such an environment, the interests of the individuals are of no consequence. The individuals must sacrifice their personal interests to the Greater Good, as manifested through the group, and, if one should put his interests ahead of it, he becomes no more nor less than one of the enemy, and a traitor to boot, who deserves to be punished in any manner possible.

And, while the anti-humanist leadership will view society as composed of two opposing groups, it will obviously view itself as representing the righteous groups against the wicked one, and it will view its role as that of subjugating the other group to itself and to its group.

But the anti-humanist leadership will hide its intentions by claiming necessity for its action, and in this process it will further consolidate its grip on society. It will do so by creating at once fear and hate in the minds of its followers, which may be done by characterizing the other groups as being wickedly engaged in plotting against itself and its group, while characterizing itself and its group as peaceful in nature but compelled, against their wish, to engage in "legitimate" self-defense against these wicked threats. The anti-humanist leadership will also consolidate its grip on society by identifying its challengers as the leaders of the wicked groups, so that it may better mobilize the people to its side against these challengers.

The anti-humanist leaders will make generous use of the labels of polarization to characterize the opposing groups and the leaders and members of these groups, so as to better emphasize the opposition between themselves and those groups.

The anti-humanist leaders will sometimes view themselves as "democratic." If these leaders happen to be leading the larger group, then they will view themselves as democratic, when this is understood to mean the majority.

The anti-humanist leaders will also view themselves as democratic when their power is so great that the majority of the people pretend to support them for fear of punishment and so that the anti-humanist leaders appear to be leading the larger group.

If, on the other hand, the anti-humanist leaders are seen to lead the smaller group, they will view democracy as "mob rule" and as an aberration, and they will characterize themselves as elitist and as anti-democratic.

But, whether the anti-humanist leaders view themselves as democratic or anti-democratic, they will have the same approach to conflicts of groups, which is to promote the polarization of society through the advent of two huge opposing and irreconcilable groups encompassing the whole of society. The humanistic leaders, on the other hand, view themselves as democratic exactly because they promote the depolarization of society through the breakdown of the larger groups until there are only small groups, which may be considered as individuals and among which it becomes possible to resolve conflicts of interest as was done between individuals, which is to endeavor to prove, in turn, that the conflicts are either illusory or unnecessary or negotiable.

Obviously, as with individuals, there will be conflicts of interest between these groups which cannot be reconciled and where the leaders will have no alternative but to use the worst method and to dictate and enforce a solution. But, in so doing, the humanistic leaders must recognize that they have achieved an imperfect solution, which is not a true democratic solution but the best substitute for such a solution under the circumstances.

As they must do for the individuals, the leaders must then do for the groups and adjudicate in favor of one or the other so as to provide the greatest satisfaction about a given need in the hope of promoting peace and security within society, and bearing in mind that many smaller dissatisfactions will add up to a large dissatisfaction. It is in this respect that it can be seen that the humanist and democratic purpose does not necessarily dictate that the leaders should satisfy the larger group when they cannot satisfy both groups. Thus it is possible that the smaller group has a greater desire of the good than the larger group and, thus, that the greater satisfaction, and possibly a greater contribution to peace and security within society, can only be achieved by satisfying the smaller group.

Again, the leaders are confronted with the problem of evaluating the desires of others, whose desires are largely subjective and private, and this problem is now magnified due to the fact that it is not only the desires of two individuals that the leaders must compare but the desires of every individual in relation to all the various groups of society.

However difficult to achieve this goal may be, the maintenance of peace and security within society through the greater satisfaction of all rather than the satisfaction of some at the expense of others, and thus the possibility of a humanist and democratic society, demands that this goal be achieved with some measure of success and that it be seen to be achieved by all concerned. And thus it is up to the humanist minister to show how and why it may be achieved and how it may be seen to be achieved.

9

THE DEMOCRATIC GOVERNMENT

It is evident that the democratic goal can be achieved and be seen to be achieved, first, in the manner that the government of society is established and maintained and, second, in the manner that it performs its role once it is established.

Then how must the democratic government be established and maintained? Humanism proposes that this must be done through a process of *democratic elections,* whereby the people choose the individuals that will serve as their leaders and that will constitute the government of society.

The democratic goal is deemed to be seen to be achieved by the process of democratic elections for no other reason than that the people feel that they are indirectly serving their feelings and desires when they partake in this process.

Of course a single election is not enough to achieve the democratic goal, since the politicians, once elected, may not perform as promised, and thus it is necessary to repeat the electoral process regularly so as to prompt the elected politicians to maintain a high standard of performance and so as to replace unsatisfactory leaders.

Having proposed that the democratic election of governments is an essential step in the achievement of the democratic goal, the humanist will be confronted by the argument that such an approach constitutes a round-about way of achieving this goal and that a more direct approach would be obviously better. Thus why do the people need leaders? Why can the people not govern themselves directly by expressing their feelings and desires, on every issue, by means of referenda? This argument seems to be reinforced by the definition of democracy. If the latter is "the government of the people by the people," then "the government by leaders" would not be a truly democratic government.

In response to these arguments, humanism proposes that the people cannot govern themselves directly without leadership and that the idea of "government *by* the people" can never mean that "the government *is* the people." Conversely, humanism proposes that the government cannot be effective and serve the people unless it remains distinct from the people. But then how can the government be "by the people"? It is because it is "elected by the people" and for no other reason. Thus the government can only be achieved indirectly "by the people" through an elected leadership.

To support its propositions, humanism must explain why a government by referenda, while producing the illusion of democracy, is in fact conducive to the establishment of the most anti-humanist and anti-democratic society possible. It is so because the rule by referenda would compel the people to be polarized on every issue. Thus every issue would be decided in favor of the majority without any possibility of evaluating the magnitude of the feelings and desires of this majority in relation to that of the minority.

The idea of government by referenda ignores the fact that individuals have many different feelings and desires, that the set of these feelings and desires is different for each individual, and that each individual attaches different importance to his various feelings and desires. The idea of government by referenda implies that all feelings and all desires are equally important for each individual and for all individuals, and it fails to recognize that each individual is ready to sacrifice the satisfaction of lesser feelings and desires in order to satisfy greater ones. This idea denies the possibility for each individual to negotiate the sacrifice of what he desires least in exchange for what he desires most. This idea disregards the fact that the people will be better satisfied if each person receives what he wants most rather than most of that which he wants. It overlooks the fact that each strong feeling or desire may be exclusive to a different minority and that the greater satisfaction of the people may then only be effected through the greater satisfaction of each minority.

(The fact that the people must not be governed by referenda does not mean that referenda must never be used within society. In fact they must be used "to constitute" the state which is to create "constitutional laws." Such laws are fundamentally different from other political laws in that they do not serve to resolve conflicts among members and groups of society, but rather they serve to delineate the rights and duties of the government and to limit its power so that it may serve rather than oppress the people. Constitutional laws are primarily contracts between the government and the governed and, as such, they ought to be approved by both parties. This is why the proclamation, amendment, and abrogation of such laws must be ratified by popular referenda.)

But what referenda cannot do, politicians can do. It is only the politicians who may listen to everyone, who may compare the subjective feelings and desires of the individuals, and thus it is the politicians, when they become leaders, who may produce the greater satisfaction even when it requires the satisfaction of the various minorities instead of the various majorities. The politicians alone can weigh the different feelings and desires and express, with more or less success, what each person desires most rather than what the majority desires.

By choosing a politician, an individual chooses a package which includes some of those things that he desires very much and which may also exclude some of those things which he desires less and which he is willing to forgo in order to obtain what he desires more. Thus it is only through the election of politicians that the people can really negotiate among themselves and thus effect a true resolution of conflicts. And this is why the popular election of political leadership is an indispensable element of the humanist and democratic society.

But all the people will not usually agree as to which politicians have the best understanding of the popular feelings and desires, and no politician can be elected by all the people. Thus, if politicians must be elected by the people, they will always be elected by the majority of the people rather than by the totality of the people. Is this fact not implying that a true democratic election is practically impossible?

Humanism proposes that a democratic election is still possible in spite of the fact that the leadership is elected by the majority rather than the totality of the people. The possibility of such an election will depend on the way that the minority views the election and its result. Of course, if the election merely serves to settle a particular conflict of interests between a well-defined majority and a well-defined minority in favor of the majority, it cannot be viewed as a truly democratic process but merely as the best substitute for such a process. But elections do not necessarily resolve particular conflicts of interest in favor of one or the other, but they may serve to select politicians that will work to achieve the resolution of many conflicts to the greater satisfaction of all the people. In such cases, the majority and the minority do not necessarily disagree on the policies that must be implemented by the politicians, but they disagree in their appraisal of the personal abilities of the different politicians to better perform the job of resolving conflicts of interest. When this is viewed to be the case by the minority, the latter will not view its own choice as critical but it will be ready to rally to the choice of the majority, once it has been expressed. And it is in this way that an election by the majority can remain truly democratic.

Ultimately, there is no way to guarantee a democratic government except if the majority wants such a government. Thus there may be circumstances when democracy will only be possible if democracy itself is one of the goods that are most desired by the majority of the people, and if this majority is willing to make a special effort to allow the minority to share in the government of society. However, if the majority and the minority are so polarized that the majority is not willing to show this kind of tolerance, then majority rule must be accepted as the best substitute for democracy, but it should not be confused with democracy.

But, if majority rule may be accepted as a substitute for democracy, minority rule should not. And yet the electoral process has often been applied so simple-mindedly that such has been the outcome. This is the case when there are more than two candidates contesting an election and where the candidate who receives the plurality of votes is deemed to be elected. It is obvious that such a candidate may be elected by a minority of the people. And yet, while such a candidate receives less than half of the votes, it is possible that another candidate may prove to be preferred by a greater number of people than this candidate. This preferred candidate, who is obviously the second and lesser choice of the greater number of voters, may in fact receive very few votes. Yet, because he is preferred by the greater number, he is the more democratic choice and he should be identified and considered elected.

Is such an election possible? It must be if the humanist and democratic ideal must be possible. And it is the duty of the humanist to propose the manner of such an election. Obviously, if the preferred candidate may be everyone's second or lesser choice, then the voters must be allowed to express such choice. Thus the democratic election demands that each voter express his order of preference among all of the candidates. Such an election is in fact a series of two-party contests, and the votes may be analyzed and translated into results about these two-party contests. Out of all such contests, one candidate will necessarily obtain the majority over all other candidates, and he represents the most truly democratic choice. It is this candidate who should be declared elected.

This approach is the only one that can guarantee meaningful electoral results when there are more than two candidates seeking election. It does so because it allows each member of society to vote in accordance with his feelings and desires without being concerned with what the other members will do. Any other electoral scheme, and particularly the scheme that restricts the voters to a single choice among all of the candidates that are running, is merely a game where candidates may be elected by accident and which will not always produce the results that are desired by the majority. The results will be further distorted because the people will endeavor to make their vote "count" by voting for their second and lesser choices, after having considered the probable election results and having guessed that their second or lesser choices have better chances of being elected than their first choices. The proposed scheme, of stating the order of preference, allows every vote to "count" and every voter is assured that he cannot affect the election results more favorably by voting contrary to his true preference.

But, more important yet, because this scheme will allow a politician to be elected in spite of the fact that he may be no one's first choice, this scheme will encourage the emergence of politicians of compromise and conciliation whose prime concern is to resolve conflicts rather than to represent one group against the others. And thus the contribution of this scheme to the promotion of the humanist and democratic society is not merely accidental but truly indispensable.

* * *

But politicians, as all human beings, have their own limitations of intelligence, knowledge, and skills. Again, large societies are so complex that few politicians can appreciate all the implications of the various factors at play within it. And this is why governments in large societies are usually effected by a number of politicians who may parcel out the tasks of government among themselves, and who may consult with each other, enlighten each other, and compensate for each other's limitations.

But those politicians who together constitute the government of a society also constitute a special society of individuals, each with his own particular beliefs and interests. And, as for every society, this one requires its own leadership, else it would destroy itself and the larger society with itself.

It is obvious that, ultimately, it is the leadership of the government which is the true leadership of society.

But, then, how is the leadership of the government established? It will necessarily be established by the politicians themselves from among their own ranks. It will be established in this manner because every politician desires to assume the leadership of society and, failing this goal, every politician hopes to have as much influence as possible on the leadership of society. Thus, while most politicians cannot achieve the leadership of society, many politicians can have a voice in the choice and a role in the support of this leadership and, as a consequence, they may exercise this influence. And they can achieve this goal by creating and joining *political parties*.

Thus political parties are a very important component of large societies, and an understanding of their nature, purpose, and potential is essential if they are to be used to promote rather than to prejudice the establishment and maintenance of the democratic government and the humanist society.

To understand the nature of political parties, we must recognize that politicians join them for one or both of two reasons. Most politicians will join such parties to satisfy their vanity by acquiring the power which they would not otherwise have, yet many will be embarrassed to admit to such an obvious reason. But all politicians claim, not always truthfully, that they participate in political activities to serve the manifest purpose of their respective parties. Thus the manifest purpose of the parties is the other reason of many politicians and the sole reason of some of the most dedicated among them.

The manifest purpose of political parties is different depending on whether or not the party is inspired by humanist and democratic ideals. The manifest purpose of the parties that are humanistic and democratic in inspiration is to offer a leadership alternative that will better serve the people, while the manifest purpose of the anti-humanist and anti-democratic parties is to represent different beliefs and to serve different groups of people at the expense of the others. In practice, no party is absolutely humanistic and democratic in inspiration, and few may be otherwise characterized as absolutely anti-humanist and anti-democratic.

Parties that are primarily democratic in inspiration because they tend to the same goal, which is to serve the people, will tend to have policies which are similar, but yet not identical, to one another's. Their difference will be in the individuals that lead these parties and in the personal style and viewpoint of this leadership.

Parties that are primarily anti-democratic in inspiration because they each tend to promote a particular and different set of beliefs, or to serve a particular and different group within society, will tend to have very different policies from each other's. Since the policies of these parties is designed to serve particular sets of beliefs or particular groups of individuals, the policies will not be dictated by the popular will. The leaders of these parties will not be valued for their style of leadership and their understanding of the popular will but for their dedication to the cause. These leaders will not be meant to put their personal stamp on the policies of the parties but they will be meant to implement the policies that have been developed and dictated by party committees that were created to guard the purity of the faith. These leaders will be meant to serve rather than lead their parties, and as such they will be weak.

But the leadership of anti-democratic parties will be weak only when the parties are out of power. As soon as one of these parties acquires the leadership of society, and because it will subscribe to the idea that it represents Absolute Goodness, it will initiate the suppression of its opposition. This party will grant more and more power to its leaders to carry out this suppression. But, as these leaders acquire this power, they will identify their persons with their cause and they will be able to use this power to suppress all opposition, including the opposition within the party. As a result, these leaders will acquire absolute power within the party and within society.

Supporters of anti-democratic parties, because they view society as polarized, will assume that every member of society must have a party affiliation, while the supporters of democratic parties will expect that the people are generally independent of party affiliation and capable of shifting their support from one party to the other. Supporters of anti-democratic parties will view such shifts of support as some kind of treason; they will assume that individuals have fixed political views and that individuals with identical or similar views or purposes should logically unite into one single party, and they will consider the plurality of democratic parties as absurd.

The supporters of anti-democratic parties will accuse the democratic parties of lacking principles. They will do so because they confuse principles and policies, and so they will fail to recognize the principle of the democratic parties, which is to give to the people what the people want, whatever that may be. The democratic parties seem to be without principles because they will adjust their policies to reflect their latest appraisal of the popular will and so as to improve their popular support. But, in so doing, they are always acting in accordance with their principle.

The principle and the policies of the anti-democratic parties are not to give the people what the people want, but to convince or to compel the people to want and to have what they will give it. And this is why, in a truly democratic society, the anti-democratic parties are at a disadvantage. Unless the people are greatly polarized, the people will be inclined to support democratic parties rather than anti-democratic parties.

When the anti-democratic parties are too weak to suppress their opposition, they will have recourse to the democratic electoral process but they will be impatient with it. Since they consider that they represent the "true beliefs" and the "righteous cause," they will consider their failure at the polls as a proof that the process is not functioning correctly. They will propose "improvements" to this process, such as the suggestion that parties should be represented in the government in proportion to their popular support. These parties will claim that proportional representation is fairer to the different parties, but their hope is that no other party will obtain the majority of support so that they may themselves participate in a government of coalition and, thus, so that they may be able to impose some of their views on society in spite of their weakness.

Humanism proposes that it is meaningless to claim that proportional representation is fairer to political parties, since such parties deserve nothing from the people and since they exist only to serve the people. Humanism further proposes that the concept of proportional representation is contrary to the popular interests, because such a scheme cannot be implemented while allowing the people to state the order of preference among the various politicians that are seeking to be elected to the government.

The scheme of proportional representation will not allow the voters to have political independence, but it will compel everyone to become partisans. This scheme will demand that the people vote for political parties rather than individual politicians. Humanism proposes that it is not the purpose of the electoral system to dictate to the people how they should vote but that it is up to each individual member of society to decide how he will vote. And a truly democratic electoral system would give him the opportunity to decide. Thus it is up to the voter to decide whether he will support a candidate because of the latter's party affiliation, or else whether he will support a party because of the candidate that is affiliated with it, or even whether he will support a candidate without affiliation.

Of course, when parties are elected through individual candidates, it is possible and probable that different politicians will be elected that belong to different political parties and thus, in an environment where there are more than two parties, it is possible that no party will obtain the majority. Such results have been interpreted as meaning that "the people did not want a majority government" and as implying that the people were directing the government to perform as a *government of coalition* or as a *minority government.*

Humanism proposes that this interpretation is simplistic and that coalitions and minority governments are as adverse to the humanist and democratic ideal as governments by referenda or as governments by proportional representation. Indeed, proportional representation of the political parties in the government could lead to coalition and minority government.

A coalition or minority government is adverse to the humanist and democratic ideal because it defeats the purpose of the democratic election. Different parties exist because of differences of principles, policies, and styles between the politicians, and the purpose of the democratic election is to allow the people to resolve these differences by choosing the party and the politicians whose characteristics most conform to the popular ideal. To recognize a coalition or minority government after the election is to claim that the people have failed to express their choice, and it is to ask the parties to do after the election what they could not do before the election, which is to resolve their differences.

Of course parties can never agree to resolve these differences, else they would be admitting that they have no reason to exist as separate entities. The ambitions of politicians would forbid such a solution, and therefore coalition and minority governments are governments in the grip of insoluble conflicts. As such, they are governments without their own leadership and, for this reason, they cannot provide leadership for society at large; they are not truly governments but the ghosts of governments, and the people can only be dissatisfied and frustrated by their weakness and instability.

Thus it is in the interest of the people that the results of the election be interpreted so as to produce a strong and stable government.

Such a strong government is only possible if one party is given a clear mandate to lead, and a strong democratic government demands that the leading party be the one which is preferred by the majority of the people. Of course such a government must be considered to be the most democratic because it is preferred by the majority, and not necessarily because it is inspired by humanist and democratic ideals. In fact, there may be other parties which are far more so inspired than the preferred party but which have failed to be elected to constitute the government. In such cases, humanism must recognize that society is severely polarized and that the election of the less humanistically and democratically inspired party is not a truly democratic result but the best substitute for such a result which is possible in the circumstances. And the humanist must accept these results knowing that nothing can be done to improve the government until something is done first to change the people by depolarizing them.

But, then, how must the preferred party be determined and how must it be given a clear mandate to lead? Humanism proposes that it is possible to analyze and interpret the election results, as must be done for individual politicians, to determine the party which is preferred by the majority of the people. And, just as the individual politician who may be no one's first choice may be preferred by the majority, so it may be for a party. In fact, the party that is preferred may not be the party with the greatest number of elected members; and this is true even in a two-party contest. And yet this party, which is preferred to every other party by the majority of the people, deserves to govern alone, and it is in the interest of the majority that it should govern alone, and without having to beg for the support of other parties.

And how should it govern alone if and when it does not have the plurality of the representation in the government? Humanism suggests that this may be achieved by weighting the power of its members that have been elected to participate in the government so that the power of this party is greater, by a comfortable margin, than the combined power of the elected members of the other parties.

Of course the fact that this party must govern alone does not mean that this party should ignore the members of the other parties that were elected to partake in the government of society. In fact, the party in power, particularly if it is inspired by humanist and democratic ideals, should consult and negotiate with these other parties and their members as much as possible. However, it should not be held to ransom by these parties but it must be capable of acting decisively whenever it deems it necessary.

10

THE HUMANIST STATE

Having considered how a government may be seen to achieve the democratic goal through the manner in which it is established and maintained, we must now consider how a government may be seen to achieve this goal through the manner in which it performs once it is established.

In fact, we touched upon this matter when we described the nature of the humanistic leadership and the meaning of democracy, which is, as we have explained, to resolve conflicts of interest to the satisfaction of all the people, and not merely of some of the people, even though these were the majority. We particularly considered this matter when we suggested that the humanistic leadership should endeavor to resolve true conflicts of interest by dividing the good so that each party may do, with his share, as he wishes and without having to consult and agree with anyone else.

But, among the goods that must be divided, there is one which demands special consideration, in particular from the humanistic leadership. To understand this fact, we must understand that everything that is, including oneself, may be a good to oneself and to others. But, while the good, which is oneself, may be just another good to everyone else, and while it may even be a liability to them, it is more than just a good to oneself. To oneself, one is the ultimate good. And thus, if the humanistic leadership must provide the greatest good to everyone, then it must provide every possible opportunity so that every member of society may enjoy the greatest good, which is oneself.

But, then, how is one to enjoy oneself unless one is free to dispose of oneself so as to serve one's feelings and desires? And this is why humanism proposes that the democratic goal can only be achieved and be seen to be achieved if the state, which is the government together with all the instruments of government, is unequivocally dedicated to one purpose, which is the promotion of the greatest possible freedom, for each member of society, to act independently of everyone else, including the state itself.

But, having thus expressed the ideal of the humanist and democratic state, we must now recognize that this state, like any other state, cannot function without imposing some obligations upon its subjects and some limitations upon their right to act freely. But the difference between the humanist and democratic state and the anti-humanist and anti-democratic state is that the former does so reluctantly and while trying to avoid doing so as much as possible.

As for every other state, the humanist state will impose itself for one or both of two reasons: it will do so to seek services from its subjects, so as to be better able to perform its own role, or else it will do so for political reasons to satisfy the needs of some members of society at the expense of the others.

But, as the humanist state seeks the services of its subjects, it must endeavor to do so as painlessly as possible, which is to respect one's greatest good which is one's person. Thus the humanist state must endeavor to tax property rather than to mobilize persons to its service. And, having done so, the humanist state may then do as any member of society must do, which is to obtain the services that it requires by buying them in the marketplace.

But some special services, such as that of obtaining the testimony of witnesses in court, cannot be obtained from the marketplace, and the state must compel those who are accidentally capable of providing these services to do so. But, when it must compel others to serve its purpose, the humanist state must endeavor to make it so that the persons who must provide the services will be willing rather than unwilling to cooperate with the state. And the humanist state may achieve this end by providing such generous compensation that the individuals who have been imposed upon will be glad to have been imposed upon.

But, there is one service which is so onerous that the state will not be able to obtain it from the marketplace, nor be able to compensate those upon whom it must impose it. Such is the military service in times of war. In such a case, the humanist state will not be able to provide more than a large yet inadequate compensation. And this compensation may be further limited because the subjects of the state will object to a greater compensation. And they will object because it is they who, as taxpayers, must ultimately provide the goods that will constitute this compensation.

But, then, is the imposition of a tax upon the members of society not demanding a service of them? And should the humanist state not compensate for this service? It is obvious that the payment of taxes is one service which can never be compensated; since it is demanded to compensate, it cannot logically be compensated.

It is also obvious that the state must only compensate when it requires the services of some rather than of all and that the state cannot compensate when it requires the same service of everyone, else it would be performing the futile and absurd exercise of compensating everyone at the expense of everyone.

Having considered that the humanist state must impose itself upon its subjects to obtain the services that it needs, we must now consider the second reason that this state would impose itself, which is to satisfy some members of society at the expense of others.

These individuals may themselves have one or both of two reasons to desire such a state intervention. They may do so to impose a behavior upon others, else they may do so to obtain a good from others to satisfy their needs. Each of these two reasons demands a very different kind of state intervention. It is important that we consider how the humanist and democratic purpose may be better served in each of these interventions.

It is necessary that the state control the behavior of the members of society for the simple reason that one cannot often act without affecting others. As these others may often find such behavior more or less objectionable and may be provoked to react violently because of it, it is in the interest of social peace that the state intervene. Yet, when the state does so, it is limiting the use of that most precious property which one is to oneself. This is why the humanist state must endeavor to intervene in a way which will grant to each member of society the opportunity to behave as he wishes as much as possible, while sparing others the experience of such behavior. And the humanist state will achieve this goal to a large extent by granting to every individual or group of individuals the right to dispose of places which are relatively private which will serve as refuges where he or they may invite anyone whom he or they may wish to invite, or from where he or they may bar or expel anyone whom he or they may wish to bar or expel, and where he or they may do those things that he or they may wish to do and which he or they may do privately and without affecting others.

Of course the humanist state may not always be able to respect the right of individuals to behave as they may wish in their privacy. Thus it is quite possible that some members of society will object to such behavior, because their feelings will not allow them to tolerate such behavior even though they may have no experience of it. These people may have enough political strength and single-mindedness to compel the humanist state to restrict the right to one's person even in one's privacy. But in complying with these demands, the humanist state must explain its own predicament to the victims of these limitations.

In fact, there is a reason that is valid even to the humanist state for invading such refuges, thereby limiting their privacy. It is to ensure that those who have entered these refuges remain willing to stay and that they have not become captives within them. And this is particularly true with respect to children who may easily be terrorized to remain in such places where they may be brainwashed to hate and to fear mindlessly so that they become a danger to society at large.

Having recognized a limited right to private refuges, the humanist state may then regulate the behavior of the people in those places which are public, which are those places which everyone is allowed to use. Thoroughfares figure prominently among these places. But every location where services are provided to the public are also such places. The state must regulate behavior in public places so as to satisfy the majority and ensure that it is not offended by the behavior of a minority. The state must also regulate behavior in public places to ensure that everyone may have access to them in peace and security. Thus the state should particularly forbid that individuals be harassed or intimidated in those places.

Of course, between the public places and the private places, there are places which offer specialized services to particular publics, and which are properly semi-private places. Each of these places should only be subjected to those regulations of the state which do not interfere with the particular service provided therein, which service is acceptable to its particular public.

Having considered why and how the humanist state may impose itself to control the behavior of the members of society, we must now consider how it must impose itself to satisfy the needs of some at the expense of the others.

When some individuals demand that the state satisfy their needs at the expense of others, they are demanding a redistribution of the wealth within society. This redistribution may be demanded because of the imbalance of wealth created by the greater ability of some individuals to produce the wealth which others envy. This redistribution may otherwise be demanded because of some special need which can only be satisfied at the expense of others.

The extent of this redistribution of the wealth will be dictated by the popular will, but a wise people and a wise government would not effect a redistribution which would unduly stifle the creation of such wealth.

But, however the humanist state may redistribute the wealth, it must not impose on one particular individual or group of individuals the duty to serve the special needs of another individual or group of individuals. Thus the goods to satisfy these particular needs must be obtained from the marketplace using the fiscal revenues which may or may not have been obtained from those who will provide the goods. In fact, the humanist state should not redistribute specific goods to satisfy special needs but, rather, this state should provide money to those whom this state considers to be in need, so that the recipients may determine themselves, according to their particular feelings and desires, what constitutes their greatest needs and so that they may buy the goods that would satisfy such needs. Thus the humanist state should only redistribute the wealth in terms of money and, by this means, it must effect the redistribution most impersonally and while providing the greatest possible freedom to both the taxpayers and the welfare recipients.

The possibility of redistributing the wealth through taxation may be limited with respect to monopolies or quasi-monopolies which may be capable of increasing their prices to compensate for the taxes, thereby circumventing the purpose of the taxation. It is apparent that, in those cases, the state should impose price controls rather than taxes, or in addition to taxes. It must be mentioned here that these monopolies may be labor unions as well as industrial corporations, and that the price controls may in fact be more precisely wage controls.

But, whether or not the humanist state redistributes the wealth, or once it has redistributed it, when it does, it must protect the ownership of this wealth with all of its might and with every means at its disposal, and it must not allow some individual or group of individuals to impose himself or themselves upon another to limit the latter's freedom and to constrain him in the use of his wealth. In fact, the humanist state must consider itself responsible for the actions of everyone against the person and his property and must endeavor to provide such generous compensation, in case of aggression, that the victim will be glad to have been victimized. (Of course there are damages, such as personal injuries, that can never be compensated and the state should not allow absurd compensations that would further tax the people without further relieving the injuries.) But, then, the humanist state, having assumed the responsibility of the aggressor, and having compensated the victim, must impose upon the aggressor the obligation to reimburse the costs of the compensation.

But, if the humanist state must protect the individual and his property from the aggression of others who would take his property or limit his freedom, it must allow this individual to dispose of his property through trade and rental and to limit his own freedom through contracts of service. It must do so because it is often in the interest of the individual to enter into such trade and contracts and the state would in fact be limiting individual freedom if it would not allow the individual to dispose of his property or to limit his own freedom.

And, with respect to contracts, the humanist state must do more than allow them. It must become a party to these contracts. This is so because these contracts will only be worthwhile if they are honored by the related parties, and a party will not enter into contract unless it is assured that the other party will be compelled to honor his promises. And only the state can ensure that such contracts are respected. Thus, if the humanist state is to help individuals create goods for themselves through contractual arrangements, it must be ready not only to allow contracts but to enforce them.

But contracts, when they engage persons rather than property, constitute a form of servitude. The state, in compelling the individuals to comply with the terms of their contracts, would therefore be imposing servitude. How can the humanist state live up to its mission of promoting personal freedom while enforcing compliance of the parties to their contracts? Should the humanist state not recognize that these contracts may prove to be distressful and would this state not better promote personal freedom by giving individuals a chance to change their minds?

Yes, the humanist state must do so and it will do so if it stipulates that contracts of service must not be absolute and if, as a party to these contracts, this state imposes its own conditions upon the contracts that it will recognize as valid and that it will accept to enforce. And the condition that the humanist state will require of most contracts is that they protect the freedom of the persons in the form of an *"escape clause."* Thus such a contract must contain a clause that expresses an amount of monetary compensation, or some other compensation in kind, that a party must pay to the other party if he wishes to default in his obligation to fulfill the terms of his contract of service. Thus the individual may choose to fulfill his contract of service, else he must accept to pay the alternative penalty or to have some or all of his assets seized to compensate for his default.

But what if he does not own sufficient assets to provide this compensation? In such cases, the humanist state must determine the cause of this insufficiency and decide in consequence. If the other party was aware that this insufficiency existed, or may have existed, then this other party accepts the risk that the first party may not fulfill his obligation and he must accept the loss without expecting that the state will enforce compensation for the default. If, on the other hand, the defaulting party misled the other party about his ability to pay, or if he intentionally lost the ability which he had when he entered into contract, then the humanist state must consider his action as reprehensible and it may very well compel him to fulfill his contract as a penalty for his action.

But what about contracts that fail to express a default compensation? Should the humanist state merely consider these contracts as invalid or should this state consider these contracts as demanding fulfillment without possibility of defaulting compensation?

The humanist state will certainly allow the last kind of contract. It will do so because there are rare instances where the value of the contract is negated by the option of defaulting. This is certainly the case with the enlisted soldier, when he is ordered into combat. Thus, many individuals could enlist to collect the pay in peacetime, with the intention of opting out if and when a war is declared. It is obvious that such an option would negate the possibility of maintaining effective standing armies. Thus the humanist state must allow contracts with no default option, but all such contracts must be subjected to a special approval by the state, which must ensure that the contracting parties are fully aware of their absolute obligation.

But, then, what about contracts which have no default option and which have not been approved by the state? Obviously, the state should not recognize such contracts as absolute. But the state should not necessarily consider these contracts as invalid. Thus, about such contracts, the humanist state must determine if a default compensation is justified at all, in which case it will adjudicate the amount of this compensation.

* * *

If the people are to enjoy the greatest possible freedom while being subjected to limitations by the state, then it is important that they be fully aware of these limitations. And the people may be so aware through laws. And this is why the humanist state must govern through clearly promulgated political laws.

As we have seen, all laws are predictions and political laws are predictions made by politicians about the actions of those who are subjected to the desires of these lawmakers. We have also seen that a political law is not valid unless the lawmaker can administer a punishment to the subject who fails to comply with the terms of the law.

Then what must be the laws of the humanist state and what must be its punishment?

The laws of any state are designed to express the method whereby this state will fulfill its purpose. And, since the purpose of the humanist state is to resolve conflicts of interest and since its preferred method is to divide the goods so that each individual may do as he pleases with his share and without having to consult and agree with anyone else, then it follows that the primary purpose of the laws of the humanist state will be to delineate the personal and property rights that are necessary to achieve this end.

Of course the humanist state cannot always fully achieve its purpose. This is so because there are many goods that cannot be fully divided, either because of their nature or because the people will not allow them to be divided. And, about these goods, the humanist state must endeavor to make laws that will divide them as much as is possible in the circumstances, which is to delineate the rights of everyone about them.

Such is the nature of the political laws of the humanist state. And it is obvious that lawbreaking in a humanist state will consist mostly in failing to respect the division of the goods and the delineated rights.

Then what about the punishment that must be expressed in these laws so as to prevent lawbreaking?

To understand the nature of this punishment we must recognize that the laws of the humanist state may only exist to serve the people and that lawbreaking is such only because it victimizes either someone or other within society or society as a whole. Then it is logical that the punishment of the laws should endeavor to repair this damage. And, to do so, the laws of the humanist state must express, as a punishment, the compensation that must be paid to the victimized individual or individuals whenever someone does not act as prescribed in relation to a good. And, when no one may be particularly identified as the victim, then society as a whole must be considered as the victim and the lawbreaker must pay compensation to the state in the form of a fine. As such, the laws are contracts which the humanist state imposes upon the people, and the punishment constitutes the equivalent of the defaulting compensation that should be expressed as an essential clause of those contracts that the humanist state will accept to enforce.

Thus the humanist state will not seek to "punish" the lawbreakers so as to serve a feeling of revenge but rather to compel them to compensate their victims in such a manner that the latter will consider themselves lucky to have been victimized.

However, many damages cannot be truly compensated. All willful or impulsive violence or threat of violence against persons and property, as well as thievery, cannot be truly compensated because they cause personal injuries. These injuries are sometimes physical, but they are always psychological. They are injuries to the intended victim, but they are also injuries to anyone who recognizes that he is also threatened by such actions.

Obviously, the humanist state must endeavor to prevent such injurious lawbreaking as much as to seek compensation. But often the state will not be able to do so. However, the state can prevent a repetition of lawbreaking. Thus, as much as obtain compensation, it must ensure that the lawbreakers will not have another opportunity to break the law and to injure members of society.

Whether the humanist state will respond to injurious lawbreaking with a feeling of vengeance demanding a cruel punishment will ultimately depend on the will of the people. The state itself must not have feelings of its own and does not seek such a response but would rather dissuade the people from compelling it to do so.

In a like manner, the state will not feel compassion for the lawbreaker. It will not consider other reasons than self-defense for justifying willful violence and threats of violence and it will never tolerate impulsive violence or threats of violence or thievery.

It will not consider that the origins or past life of the individual or his present circumstances, such as poverty, can serve as an excuse and a justification for injurious lawbreaking. The humanist state has the overwhelming duty to provide peace and security to the people, and it cannot do so if it tolerates individuals who will make attempts against this peace and security. This is why it must progressively remove these individuals from society until society contains only those individuals who are willing to respect this peace and security. It must remove them from society also for the reason that their presence within society constitutes an enticement for others to break the law, as they have done.

It must remove them without feelings either of antipathy against them or of compassion for them. It must remove them for only one purpose, which is to provide the greatest peace and security within society. Of course the people may have feelings of antipathy or compassion and they may impose these feelings upon the state, and the state must implement the popular will that follows from such feelings while itself remaining indifferent to these feelings.

Then how should these individuals be removed from society? Obviously, the easiest method is to execute them. But this approach is not without problems. It is possible that an individual may be executed who may later be exonerated. And the people must recognize that this possibility constitutes a threat to every individual in society. And it is to remove this possibility that the people may prefer to see condemned individuals jailed rather than executed, particularly when they have been condemned on the basis of circumstantial evidence, which evidence may prove less reliable in the future than it appears in the present.

But some people will feel compassion for condemned individuals, and they will demand that all of them, regardless of circumstances, be jailed rather than executed.

But then the maintenance of jails, in lieu of executions, constitutes an extra financial burden upon society. And the maintenance of jails may be a cause of conflict within society between those who favor this approach for reasons of compassion and those who favor executions as a means of saving public funds.

It is to resolve this conflict that a third option may be suggested which would not entail executions or a costly financial burden upon society. It is that condemned individuals be banished to penal colonies where they may lead more normal lives, away from the main society and while contributing to their own society, which could be more self-sustaining and less of a burden than jails on the public funds. And, inasmuch as jailing constitutes a harsher punishment than banishment to penal colonies, the latter option is preferable, at once, to those who feel compassion for the condemned individuals and to the humanist state which will have avoided imposing a more cruel punishment.

But, if penal colonies are to serve their purpose, which is to remove injurious lawbreakers from society at the least cost, then these penal colonies must be able to retain the banished individuals without demanding costly security measures. To do so, the management of these colonies must endeavor to discourage their inhabitants from attempting to escape to the main society. It must achieve this end by imposing a severe penalty for escaping to the main society while removing as much as possible the temptation of such escape.

To ensure that individuals are not greatly tempted to escape to the main society, the humanist state must ensure that individuals may live in peace and security within the colonies. Thus the humanist state must do everything to prevent lawbreaking within these colonies, as it must do for society at large.

To ensure that lawbreaking is maintained at a minimum, the state must remove recidivists from the penal colonies. Whether it should condemn these recidivists to special penal colonies, or to jail, or to execution, or whether it should condemn them in turn to these progressively more severe punishments as they continue to repeat their acts, is a matter to be decided according to the will of the people; but, whatever is done, the main penal colony, or colonies, must be rid of crime as much as possible so that its inhabitants may live in peace and security.

To further reduce the temptation to escape from the penal colonies, the humanist state should endeavor not to compel individuals coming from very different criminal backgrounds into the same penal colony, where they may live in fear of each other. Thus the humanist state should create different penal colonies which would harbor individuals according to the kind of crimes that they are alleged to have committed. As a minimum, there should be a penal colony dedicated to individuals who were found guilty of committing violent acts or threats of such acts against persons and there should be another penal colony for individuals who are deemed to have committed crimes against property. There should also be different colonies for those who are found guilty of such acts on the basis of circumstantial evidence, particularly if they claim to be innocent.

Having taken these precautions against the temptation of escaping from the penal colonies, the humanist state must deal harshly with those who would escape or attempt to escape from these colonies. The humanist state may apply at least the same penalties as it would to recidivists within the colonies. It might even consider that these individuals were condemned to penal colonies in lieu of the death penalty and therefore that an escape deserves no less than an automatic death penalty.

If individuals should not be allowed to escape from penal colonies, neither should they usually ever be released from them. To understand this policy, it is necessary to consider the reason for incarceration and banishment. If individuals are condemned to these punishments to prevent them from repeating their illegal acts, then it is logical that the condemnation should not be limited but should be in perpetuity.

This does not mean that the state may never release some individuals from the penal colonies to allow them to return to the main society. There will certainly be compassionate people who will demand such releases and who may impose their will upon the state. But such releases must never constitute a right of the condemned individuals. The state will then release those individuals when, in its judgment, it is reasonably sure that they have lost their propensity to break the law. And the state ought to maintain a particular surveillance of these individuals once they are released.

* * *

But, before an individual may be condemned, he must first be found out, and the circumstances of the crime must be established so that he may be accused of lawbreaking; and he must then be given an opportunity to defend himself from this accusation.

The first stage of this process is incumbent on the police force of the state. And, if the police force must perform effectively, find out lawbreakers, and elucidate circumstances, then it must dispose of powers which are not available to other individuals within society. And this fact must be cause for concern to the humanist state. It is cause for concern because members of police forces are individuals with their own interests and they may be tempted to use their power to serve these interests contrary to the interests of the people. And it is to prevent such abuses that the power of the police force in the humanist state must be balanced with guarantees against these abuses.

And the most important of these guarantees will consist in a review, after the fact, of every instance where the police force has used power which other individuals are not entitled to use, and this review should determine if there were abuses. But, even while it uses such power, the police force must be subjected to strict procedures so as to prevent abuses as much as possible.

The duty and privilege of the police force in seeking out culprits, when lawbreaking has occurred, will consist in carrying out surveillance of suspects, in questioning presumed witnesses, and in searching private property. It is such surveillance, questioning, and searches which may be occasions of abuses and harassments. To reduce the possibilities of these abuses and harassments, the authority of the police force to watch, question, and search must be limited by the gravity of the lawbreaking under investigation. Thus it must be more limited or even sometimes forbidden when the lawbreaking does not imply injury. Then, questioning should be held in circumstances similar to a judicial court and surveillance and searches should have to be authorized by judicial authorities, and every possible record must be obtained and maintained of the police activity so that it may be later examined and judged as to its appropriateness.

However, the police force may not always be capable of performing its duty if it is to follow all of the established procedures, because there are circumstances when it cannot be effective unless it acts urgently and secretly. This is why the police force must be allowed to bypass the required procedures when it may prove that it is necessary to the performance of its duty. But all such actions must be revealed within a reasonable time and must be particularly considered in the review, after the fact, of the police action, to determine if they were truly justified and to remedy any abuse.

The police force must also be allowed to use its power to prevent some lawbreaking rather than merely to detect such lawbreaking. But such a privilege must be even more limited and must apply only to serious injurious lawbreaking, particularly in instances of organized criminal activity.

All individuals who must cooperate with the police force in their inquest and who are importuned by their surveillance and searches, whether knowingly or not, must be compensated to the extent that they are not found to share responsibility for the offense under investigation. This compensation must be greater if the police force bypassed the applicable procedures and to the extent that these procedures were bypassed. This compensation must be greater yet to the extent that the police force is ultimately judged not justified in having bypassed these procedures. On the other hand, individuals who fail to cooperate with the police force in their inquest and search and fail to provide the necessary information to prevent and detect lawbreaking must be considered to be accomplices of the lawbreakers and must share in the penalty.

But, once the police force has identified a lawbreaker and gathered evidence against him, the individual is not yet condemned. Thus, before the individual is condemned, the humanist state must do everything in its power to ensure that the individual is not innocent in spite of the evidence, and the individual must be given the opportunity to defend himself. This is more important because the police force, in the performance of its duties, has become a party that has an interest in proving that it has succeeded in this performance. This is why the evidence must be publicized and reviewed by a judiciary, independent of the police force, having no interest in proving that the evidence is valid. But the judiciary itself can be an occasion of abuse, and it is important to develop the rules that must govern the performance of the judiciary so as to reduce the chance of abuse and ensure that individuals are not judged and condemned haphazardly.

However, it is not always possible to avoid penalizing an individual even before a judgment is rendered. This is the case with respect to injurious lawbreaking when those who have committed such offenses may be expected to repeat them while awaiting trial, or may go into hiding if they expect to be found guilty. Thus it is necessary to ensure that the accused does not have these opportunities. To provide this insurance, it is necessary to arrest the individual that is so accused. But the state must remember that this arrest is performed primarily for the convenience of the state itself and that the individual, in his arrest, is asked to provide a service to the state. This is why the state must apply strict rules to govern such arrests and to provide compensation if the individual is exonerated. Thus every effort must be taken to protect the arrested individual against police abuse. Thus the police force should ensure, as much as possible, that third parties are present to witness the arrest and that the captive is never left alone with his captor, where he may be at his mercy. The captive must be maintained in comfortable quarters where he may receive visitors to witness his incarceration and where he may enjoy as much as possible the amenities of ordinary society.

Every police arrest must eventually be judged as to its justification and propriety. Every arrest which does not lead to a conviction must be generously compensated. In addition, every arrest which is judged not justified by the circumstances must be liable for substantial extra compensation. Finally, every arrest when the police force has abused the victim must demand yet further substantial compensation, while the guilty police officer must be liable to provide this compensation, as well as liable to criminal responsibility. In this respect, a police officer who fails to take the necessary measures to ensure that the arrest and captivity are witnessed and recorded as much as possible must be deemed guilty of having committed the abuses of which he would be accused.

The procedures of judicial courts must be such that the accused individuals and the witnesses are not abused by the circumstances of the courts. The state must ensure that the courtrooms are equally comfortable to everyone present. The fact that the court procedure consists in the questioning of witnesses, often in an adversary environment, provides many opportunities for the abuse of these witnesses. To ensure that such abuses do not occur, the witness may demand that the questions be addressed to the judge, who must consider each question to determine if it is justified and who must reword it, if necessary, to remove any offensive wording or tone of voice before addressing it to the witness.

The accused may defend himself in one or more different ways. The first line of defense is to claim that the accusation is invalid, either because it is worded in meaningless or self-contradictory terms or because it fails to refer to an existing nonretroactive law. If the judge recognizes that this is the case, then he must reject the accusation. It is only when the accused admits that this is not the case, or when the judge refuses to recognize that this is the case, that the accused may withdraw to his second line of defense, which is to claim that the law itself is invalid because it is worded in meaningless or self-contradictory terms.

To understand why it is necessary to judge the validity of the accusation and the law, it is necessary to remember that these are statements and that, as such, they constitute a use of language. It is because language may be misused and abused that it is possible that they be invalid. Thus the judge must consider if the law is meaningless or self-contradictory, in which case he must declare the law invalid and absolve the accused of any possible guilt.

This procedure must be true of any state. But the humanist state must do more with respect to the law: in such a state, the judge must ensure that the law serves to resolve conflicts between individuals. And, for this purpose, the law itself must not be, by its very wording, a source of conflict. And the law will be such a source of conflict if its meaning is subjective. Thus the judge in a humanist state must ensure that the laws have an objective meaning and must recognize that any law that fails this criterion is invalid.

A law has an objective meaning when it commands an act whose meaning is the same for everyone, whose meaning is not dependent on one's particular feelings. The meaning of the law and the act that it commands or forbids must be clear and must not require to be defined or interpreted by the judge. Thus an individual may interpret as he pleases a law that requires interpretation, and the judge must accept this interpretation as valid. If the judge were to interpret the law contrary to the individual, and if he were to resolve the case according to his own interpretation, the judge would be legislating by creating retroactive laws!

This is why the judge must render his judgment according to the terms of the law, and thus he must not seek out the "intention of the legislator." The law is always deemed to express *what the legislator intended,* and if the legislator failed to express himself adequately then he has created an invalid law and the judge must recognize this fact rather than seek the alleged "spirit of the law," which is deemed to lie "beyond the letter of the law."

But the law of the humanist state must be more objective than in meaning alone: it must command or forbid objective acts. It must not command or forbid feelings or desires or even thoughts. It must not command or forbid to love or to believe. Nor must it command that an objective act be accompanied by a feeling. It must not demand such because it would be demanding the impossible: one can choose to perform an objective act, but one cannot choose to love or not to love, to believe or not to believe. In fact, in the humanist state, what one feels or thinks or desires is no one's business but one's own and must never be the subject of laws or inquiries by the state.

It is only after the accused has accepted that the accusation is valid and that the law upon which it is based is also valid, or that the judge has rejected his arguments that they are not so, that he will consider his third line of defense, which is that he has not committed the act of which he is accused or that he has committed it but not willfully or impulsively.

In this respect, it is up to the state to prove that the act was committed and it not up to the defendant to disprove that he has committed the act. However, once the state has proved that the act was committed it is not up to the state to prove that it was willful or impulsive, but it is up to the individual to prove that it was not so. This is so because every individual is deemed to act willfully or impulsively and the individual is best capable of explaining that he did not.

And it is up to the judge to consider the "proofs" or claims before him and to decide if he "finds" the defendant "guilty" or "not guilty" of having committed the illegal act of which he is accused. The judge will certainly resort to his feelings about the truth of the claims before him when he must decide if one is guilty or not. But, if the judge must use his feelings to judge the claims, he must not use his feelings to judge the accused. Thus he must render his judgment without displaying emotions or feelings toward or against the accused. Thus he must judge whether one has obeyed or disobeyed the law and not whether one is "good" or "bad," "praiseworthy" or "despicable." The fact that a judge would show such emotions should be enough reason to question the competence of the judge and to appeal the judgment.

But the fact that one is "found" guilty does not mean that one has "committed" the act but merely that a judgment has been rendered to that effect. Thus the individual so judged must have the right to disagree with the judgment, to claim that the accusation or the law is invalid, or to deny that he has committed the act, or even to deny that he is "guilty" while admitting having committed the act. Furthermore, the individual must have the right to insist that others, on pain of defamatory liability, be very careful of what they report. They may report that "he has been *found* guilty" but they must not report that "he is guilty" or that "he has committed the act." The state must respect the opinion of the condemned individual about the judgment and must not demand that he "recognize his guilt." The state must accept that any judgment may be in error and it must rather be particularly respectful of those who refuse to admit their guilt when condemned on the basis of circumstantial evidence. This is so because the state is seeking a guarantee that individuals will not commit illegal acts, and the expected lawfulness of the individual who refuses to admit a guilt is greater than that of the individual who admits that he has found occasion to break the law.

The state must neutralize the condemned individual without demanding feelings of him. Thus the state must not demand "remorse" or demand that this individual confess that his act was "wrong."

Finally, it is evident that the individual who is accused of lawbreaking and acquitted must be compensated for his court costs as well as for the inconvenience of having to submit to the judicial process. Again, this compensation must be such that the individual should be glad to have been accused.

11

THE HUMANIST WORLD

Having established the identity of humanism, elaborated its philosophy, described its ministry, and demonstrated its practical application in society, we must now recognize that it has failed in the world throughout history, and we must attempt to explain this failure and to develop the ways whereby humanism may take its place in the sun.

If humanism truly represents the hope of mankind, then why is it weak and on the defensive? To understand the failure of humanism we must recognize the fact that humanism has never been able to articulate itself in an adequate manner. And it has not been able to do so because it has never been viewed as a distinct system of beliefs, whereas its competitors have never had such a problem.

We have considered that the essential difference between humanism and anti-humanism is their opposite beliefs about human nature and purpose. Thus, while humanism claims that a human being is his own purpose and that his nature is to seek the good to satisfy his needs as dictated by his feelings and desires, anti-humanism claims that a human being is not his own purpose and that it is because his nature is perverted that he seeks the good to satisfy his needs.

Then where is the anti-humanism that has the upper hand over humanism? What are the prevailing religions today?

We propose that there are three major nonhumanist religions today which are actively competing against humanism and against each other. They are Communism, Islam, and Christianity. Of these religions, only Communism is absolutely anti-humanist. This is so because only Communism offers a view of humanity as composed of individuals whose nature it is to be condemned to serve a purpose without ultimate personal satisfaction. Christianity and Islam appear to be anti-humanist, but they are not truly so. Inasmuch as these two religions propose that human purpose is to act to obtain an ultimate reward in the after-life, they are perfectly in accord with the humanist purpose. They may appear to be anti-humanist when they propose that human life should be spent in submission, suffering, and sacrifice, but they are not truly so because they believe that the ordeal of human life on earth is merely a means to a greater end, which is salvation in an after-life where there is no suffering or sacrifice.

Thus these two religions do not deny the humanist principle. They merely state that it is unimportant in the immediate and that it is only meaningful in the long run. Thus, to these religions, human nature is perverted when it seeks the lesser, earthly good rather than the greater, heavenly good, but it is not perverted to seek the latter good. The humanist must recognize that this belief is not illogical. Thus what the humanist will question is not the logic but the evidence for the Christian and Islamic beliefs. Thus the humanist will question the evidence for an after-life which justifies the sacrifice of the earthly life. Humanism will propose that the evidence for the existence of God and for the kind of God proposed by these religions is inadequate and that it considers the plausibility of such an existence as faint. As a consequence, the humanist cannot accept that his earthly life is merely a means which has no importance in itself. And this is why the humanist refuses to suffer and to sacrifice his earthly life and why he wishes to live it to the fullest according to his feelings and desires.

But, then, where in the world today is humanism opposing the major nonhumanist religions? We know of Communist and Islamic and Christian countries, but where are the humanist countries? They exist unbeknown to themselves. They are "the democracies." They are "the West." Of course these countries are not fully humanist. This is why they fail to recognize themselves for what they are. They are like humanism itself. They are afflicted with a crisis of identity. And this is why they are so vulnerable to the attacks of their adversaries.

The West has often been accused of being decadent by the Communists, the Muslims, and the Christians, and particularly by the Eastern Christians. The West has seemed unable to defend itself from this accusation. The West has welcomed the prophets from the East, has cowered before them, and has received their admonition in all humility. How is this possible? The explanation of this fact is of the utmost importance to the humanist. It is so because it reveals something about the nature of the West and something about the difference between the East and the West.

The first thing that must be said is that what these religions see as a cause of decadence in the West is in fact the presence of humanism. But the presence of humanism in the West is not like the presence of Communism or Islam or Christianity in the East. This presence is truly unrecognized by those who claim to be humanists, although it is certainly evident to those who accuse the West.

The difference between the East and the West is that humanism is tolerated in the West. And it is tolerated because *it is* the religion of the West, while not being recognized as such. Thus, while the West claims to be Christian, it is in fact humanist. In the West, both humanism and Christianity are present each in its own way, Christianity more overtly, so that the countries of the West claim to be Christian while being fundamentally humanist. This is not without creating a permanent inner conflict in the West and it is this conflict which appears to be the manifestation of decadence.

And the result of this purported decadence is deemed to be the "consumer society," the "permissive society," which is lacking the will to suffer and to sacrifice and which is therefore unwilling to defend itself and, thus, which is doomed to be conquered. But humanism denies that the West is decadent, while it denies that decadence is the unwillingness to suffer and to sacrifice. The humanist will acknowledge that a society is decadent when it refuses to suffer short-run sacrifices of lesser goods in order to obtain greater goods in the long run. And the humanist will be the first to recognize the desirability of such sacrifices. But such sacrifices are not the suffering which the humanists are accused of avoiding. The humanists are accused of avoiding, rather than seeking and welcoming, the suffering which is endured for its own sake or for the vague purpose of "toughening the will." The humanist proposes that such suffering is unnecessary. It is not because a society is ready to endure such suffering that it will be willing to defend itself, but it is rather because it is unwilling to suffer and to sacrifice and because it is capable of anger when suffering is imposed upon it and because, in this anger, it is willing to inflict greater suffering upon its tormentors.

Thus the West is not decadent and not about to collapse and surrender. To the contrary, if it were to find its humanist soul and proclaim it as it should, the superiority of the West would be such that the rest of the world would stand in amazement, as it grudgingly does already, although it refuses to admit it.

And humanism must be no less desirous of converting the world to its cause than Communism, Islam, or Christianity, because it is only in a humanist world that the humanist society will be safe and that each individual human being will better be able to live in accordance with his nature and purpose.

Humanism must seek to be the established religion. It must do so because every society is governed by a view of human nature and purpose, and if that view is not humanist it will be nonhumanist or anti-humanist. Thus every society is necessarily governed by a religious view, and it is absurd for those who claim to be humanists to seek the "separation of Church and State."

But, then, how is humanism to become the established religion? It will do so by seeking the tolerance of every religion. To understand how this tolerance constitutes the establishment of humanism, we must understand that, while humanism proposes that each individual must live in accordance with his nature and purpose by seeking the good to satisfy his needs as dictated by his feelings and desires, humanism does not dictate to the individual what these feelings and desires must be, but it recognizes that each individual may have different feelings and desires. This is not the case with nonhumanist religions that claim that all individuals should have the same feelings and desires, and these religions are prompt to spell out what those feelings and desires should be.

Humanism, when it allows the individual to live in accordance with his own particular feelings and desires, does not eliminate the possibility that the individual will adopt the feelings and desires of a particular nonhumanist religion. And this is why humanism must be tolerant of every religion, and why humanism is the established religion simply by being so tolerant. Of course these different feelings and desires may be the cause of conflicts which must be resolved by the state; but, inasmuch as there is no such conflict, humanism proposes that each individual should pursue the good that will satisfy the needs that are dictated by these different feelings and desires.

Thus, if tolerance is essential to the humanist society, then tolerance cannot constitute a threat for humanism, else humanism could not exist except as a self-contradiction. This is why humanism must be so sure of the self-evidence of its point of view that it does not need to fear that another religion can use this tolerance to overthrow humanism and to establish itself as the religion of society. Thus the humanist must have faith that, whenever his beliefs are expressed clearly, they will prevail against nonhumanism and anti-humanism. But then the great paradox of humanist tolerance is that, by imposing tolerance, humanism is imposing its religious beliefs on others and restricting the practice of their religions by limiting the exercise of their intolerance!

Thus the proof that the West is fundamentally humanist is that humanism is tolerated. If the West were fundamentally Christian, humanism would not be tolerated, as is the case in the East. Christianity, like Islam and Communism, will not tolerate opposition because its mandate is to convert the world, and this mandate is incompatible with tolerance. The very existence of Christianity depends on this intolerance. It depends on this intolerance because its beliefs would not be accepted by the majority of a people that is free to choose in an environment of vigorous humanist criticism.

The Christian has a compulsive need to impose his beliefs upon the whole world. He has this need because he believes that the salvation of all of mankind is at stake. More important, he has this need because he believes that his own salvation depends on his effort to fulfill his divine mandate to convert the world. Finally, he has this need because he feels that the existence of disbelief is an encouragement to his own disbelief and therefore that it weakens his own resolve to save himself and that, as such, it constitutes the greatest possible threat to his own well being. It is obvious that this reasoning would render tolerance into nothing more than an absurd nicety. Thus it is reasonable that Christianity should compel people to believe and to be saved, and should remove, by every possible means, those who stand in the way of this faith and this salvation. And the persecutions of history are there to prove that this is the essential policy of Christianity.

However, in the West Christianity cannot be as intolerant as it would like; it must pretend to be tolerant. And this willingness to compromise is seriously affecting its vitality. And it is this lack of vitality which Western Christians are mourning and which they confess as the decadence of their own world when they worship at the feet of the Eastern prophets and as they admire the uncompromising convictions of these prophets, who may be compelled to be tolerant but who never admit that they should be so of their own free will.

But, then, how did humanism manage to emerge from an intolerant Christian world and how did it become the religion of the West? To understand how this could come about we must understand that the first manifestations of humanism pretended to be Christian. Such was the Renaissance, which did not challenge Christianity directly but which proclaimed the value of earthly life through art which pretended to depict Christian themes and to serve the Christian cause. But the wealth and beauty of the Renaissance was a silent contradiction of the principle of the Church by distracting from the cult of poverty and suffering.

The second great boost to the humanist cause was the Reformation, which, paradoxically, emerged in reaction to the Renaissance and which was often more decidedly anti-humanist than Catholicity, particularly in the case of Calvinism, which proclaimed that individuals are predestined to salvation or damnation but that they must obey God in spite of this fact and in spite of the fact that this obedience serves no human purpose. Thus it is not the Reformation itself but the aftermath of the Reformation which proved to be a boost to humanism. Thus the tolerance of the dissidents, which became necessary at the conclusion of the indecisive wars of religion and which was consecrated by the haven of tolerance established in America, weakened Christianity and proved to be the opportunity for humanism to establish itself and to launch the Enlightenment. It is the spirit of the Enlightenment which has lasted to this day and which constitutes the presence of humanism in the West.

The reason that the presence of humanism in the West was not obvious was the emergence of a new kind of religion which appeared as a reaction to the Enlightenment and which soon monopolized attention.

What further confused the issue was that these new religions appeared to be the product of the Enlightenment. Thus this new kind of religion had its origin, during the later part of the Enlightenment, in the absurd views of Rousseau, who proclaimed that the particular will of the individual is only good when it identifies with "the General Will of the State," and he compounded this absurdity by adding that the General Will is not necessarily "the will of all." From this belief, there is only one step to the belief that human beings must not serve their own purposes but that they are destined to serve "something greater than themselves" for no other reason than that "it is their duty." It is in this manner that totalitarianism emerged on the world scene.

Of totalitarianism, there are two kinds. There is Communism, which preys on the dissatisfaction of the oppressed peoples and proclaims that human beings are the helpless pawns in a universal revolution based on class struggle. There is also Fascism, which preys on the fear of the middle class and proclaims that an individual has no value except to serve his appointed group, whether race or nation or state, and to support it against the lowly and undeserving opponents that threaten it with subversion and revolution.

Communism succeeded mainly in non-Western countries because these countries were the poorer, while Fascism had successes mainly in the West, where, because of the colonial successes of these countries, the people of these countries could, however poor they were, still consider themselves "the middle class of the world." In fact, Christianity and Fascism often fancied themselves as allies against Communism.

In hindsight, it must be said that the Western colonial successes could have been a wonderful opportunity for the promotion of humanism, but, because of its crisis of identity, the West failed to seize this opportunity. The weakness of humanism in the West, the influence of Christianity and of Fascism, and the morbid fear of Communism, led to a disastrous Western foreign policy. And this policy was disastrous particularly because it was short-sighted and negative.

Thus, while the West had established a colonial empire that could have been an ideal instrument for the spread of humanism, it then chose to send Christian missionaries to teach the colonized people to sacrifice and suffer while they were being exploited by their colonial masters. This proved to be a fertile ground for Communists, who could come to convince the people that their sacrifices and suffering should be diverted to overthrow their colonial masters. Ultimately, Western foreign policy, because of the Western conflict of identity, became exclusively anti-Communist rather than being in favor of anything. The West could not win with such a negative approach. Yet the West could not recognize and accept the absurdity of its approach. The culmination of the disaster came in Vietnam, where the Americans foolishly assumed the burden of the faltering French and where Cardinal Spellman's "Christian soldiers" set out on a crusade against "atheistic Communism." Thus the Americans went to Vietnam thinking that they could bomb and poison an idea out of the mind of a people.

The American failures in Vietnam, and later in Iran, have demonstrated the limitations of the options available to the West, which is condemned to the defensive posture of propping up unpopular regimes against popular uprisings While such a policy may be unavoidable in the short run, it is unacceptable in the long run because it is a policy that is doomed to failure. The continued success of Communism and Islam is a clear proof of this fact.

If the West must regain the initiative it must adopt a positive policy of promoting humanism and democracy. If the West has lost the opportunities that were available in colonial time, it has not lost all opportunities. Above all, the West is still capable of preaching by example, which is to constitute its own societies as the most attractive possible, where conflicts are resolved promptly and peacefully, and where individuals may live in tranquillity and security to pursue their own interests as dictated by their feelings and desires.

To do so, the West must become aware of its humanist soul and it must shed the burden of Christianity. It must replace the cult of sacrifice and suffering with the pursuit of well-being and happiness. It must replace the crucifix with the centerfold as the symbol of its ideal.

Humanism must reassure the West that it does not need to be intimidated by the likes of Solzhenitsyn, or the Ayatollah Khomeini, or Mother Teresa, or Khrushchev, or Muggeridge. Humanism must proclaim that it is reasonable to admire beauty and success without shame, and to desire and enjoy wealth without guilt, and it must tell the people that they do not need to pretend that sacrifice, poverty, and wretchedness are somehow superior to wealth and well-being, nor do they need to be impressed by the assumed superiority of those who will spend their lives suffering and sacrificing. To the humanist, these latter individuals are merely serving their strange feelings and desires in their own peculiar way and, in so doing, are deserving of no particular admiration.

* * *

But, if the West is to find its humanist soul and become conscious of its humanist heritage, and if it is to demonstrate its superiority to the world by creating the most attractive societies possible, then the humanists must be able to group themselves into effective organizations within these societies so that they may influence them and so that humanism may be unmistakably recognized as the established religion of the West. Thus it is the weakness of the humanist organizations that has particularly hindered the promotion of humanism.

Then why are humanist organizations so weak. We propose that it is because those who claim to be humanists have failed to recognize the nature and purpose of the humanist organization as much as the nature and purpose of humanism itself.

We have already explained that the weakness of humanism itself was due to a crisis of identity and that humanism was often considered either as a political belief or as humanitarianism when it is in fact a religion which has nothing to do with humanitarianism and which is above politics. We propose that the weakness of the humanist organizations may be explained in the same manner and that a religious organization cannot be managed like a political organization, as it is often tempted to do. And, whenever a religious organization, whether humanist or nonhumanist, has endeavored to be managed as a political organization, it has been torn with internal strife and weakened.

Then how should a religious organization be managed, and how is it different from a political organization? To understand this, we must first recognize the difference in purpose between the political and the religious organization. Thus, while the purpose of the political organization is to serve the interests of its members, such is not the purpose of the religious organization. The purpose of a religious organization is to promote a belief or a set of beliefs.

But, if the purpose of these two kinds of organizations are different, then the attitude and relationship of their memberships to themselves must also be different. It is self-evident that individuals join political organizations to serve their feelings and desires and that such organizations must consult their members to find out what these feelings and desires may be so that they may better serve them. But individuals do not join religious organizations to serve their feelings and desires, except indirectly. What they must serve directly are the beliefs of these organizations. And the beliefs of these organizations are not created by the organizations but it is the beliefs that serve to create the organizations. And thus the organizations cannot consult their memberships to establish their beliefs. And, if an organization attempts to do so, it admits that it has not yet found its reason to exist and that, in fact, it does not exist. This has been the case of the humanist organizations in the world to this date: they are organizations that pretend to exist but that do not exist.

Thus, in principle, there should be no disagreements about beliefs within religious organizations, and, if there should arise such disagreements, it is important to do everything possible to resolve them. But these disagreements cannot be resolved, as in political organizations, through negotiations and concessions. One cannot negotiate away one's beliefs. These disagreements must be resolved by finding the cause of the disagreements and by removing this cause. And, in cases where such a cause cannot be found, and when the disagreements persist, then it is necessary to recognize that some members should leave the organization to find a more suitable one or to create a new one which will promote their different beliefs. Ultimately, it is better to have many organizations that can each promote a clear belief than to have one organization that is divided within itself and that cannot speak meaningfully.

It is not to be expected that the multiplicity of humanist organizations should exist because of fundamental differences of beliefs about the humanist principle. If such exists, then it is to be expected that each organization would consider the others as being other than humanistic in inspiration. However, humanism must tolerate and even encourage a multiplicity of humanist organizations based on differences in style. This is possible because humanism is seeking intellectual leverage rather than political leverage. It is seeking to convince rather than to compel. And, in this way, it is very different from nonhumanist organizations and particularly anti-humanist organizations. Thus, the multiplicity of humanist organizations will constitute the rich intellectual ferment that is better capable of producing the gems of logic that will convince.

But the variety of organizations cannot come from the membership. This is so because a collectivity is incapable of intellectual activity. A collectivity cannot think or speak except in the most moronic and inarticulate manner. It is only the individual who can speak intelligently and articulately. And thus, if organizations are to be different from each other, and if they must be graced with style and color, then they must each obtain it from a particular individual. And the only individual that can affect an organization in this manner must be its leader, hence the importance of leadership to religious organizations and particularly to humanist organizations. Thus each humanist leader must imprint his own style on his organization, and this variety of organizations will not fragment and weaken humanism but it will complement and strengthen it. This is particularly so because smaller organizations will provide their members with a greater sense of purpose and would be better managed than one single giant organization that may be paralyzed by an impersonal bureaucracy and where some competent exponents of humanism would not have opportunities to contribute their talents to the promotion of their cause.

It is obvious that the leader of the humanist organization must not be chosen because of his administrative ability but because he can speak forcefully and imaginatively about humanism. Thus the greatest asset of the humanist leader, in fact his essential asset, will be his ability to speak out effectively about the misuses and abuses of language and words, which misuses and abuses lead to misunderstandings about the nature and purpose of human societies and of human beings. Individuals with these qualifications are not plentiful and organizations only can falter if they lack this kind of leadership. Thus it is the purpose of humanists to seek out these individuals as the leaders of the organizations that they will support.

And, if they must support these leaders because they recognize the latter's competence, then they cannot dictate their beliefs to these leaders but these leaders must explain to them what and why they must believe. Ultimately, the leader does not represent the organization or the membership of the organization, but he represents the beliefs of the organization. Then, if the organization exists to promote its beliefs, it follows that the organization also exists to support the leader by providing him with every possible means to better articulate these beliefs.

Thus the fundamental role of the humanist leader is to be forever present whenever the humanist principle is being challenged, and this presence must be such that it cannot be ignored.

The leader in this position must represent the people against nonhumanism and against the state. To do so, he must comment every time they fail to serve the interests of the people. Thus the people must come to expect a humanist response on every occasion where a religious principle is in question, and the nonhumanist and the anti-humanist must come to expect that they will not state their case without being challenged.

And it is in this manner that the advent of the humanist millennium will be made possible.